Esquire

THE
HANDBOOK
OF
MEN'S

Style

A GUIDE TO LOOKING GOOD

CONTENTS

FOREWORD

There are three things we must do every day: sleep, eat, and get dressed. While there is endless advice about rest and diet, sartorial matters are still underserved. And yet, the act of putting on clothes is a fundamental ritual. Which is why, for more than 90 years, Esquire has treated it with careful consideration.

This book is a distillation of that history, tuned to the modern age. It will give you the basics, tell you what not to do, and help you understand how men's style has evolved in the last decade. It should inspire you. We are in the Choose Your Own Adventure era of menswear. When men get dressed today, they have myriad choices. It can be overwhelming. This book will arm you to make those decisions so you feel confident when you leave the house.

We believe that style is serious business; we also believe that you shouldn't take it too seriously. Getting dressed should be a pleasure—as delicious as a great meal and as restorative as a good night's sleep.

Have fun,
Michael Sebastian
Editor-in-Chief, Esquire

INTRODUCTION

This book is a road map for a territory that's familiar and strange at the same time. The landscape of style is forever shifting, but these days that change is happening at a dizzying pace, as disparate forces from technical advancements to ecological consciousness to an evolving definition of masculinity collide in a crucible with weird and wonderful results. Mindful that change is the only constant, we'll show you the lay of the land, point out the latest attractions, warn against the proverbial tourist traps, and send you on your way with a recalibrated sense of direction and a willingness to sample everything you encounter.

Our mantra is that you don't need more clothes; you need better clothes. These chapters offer advice on how to acquire the finest-quality gear you can afford. They also explain why these pieces work well together and suggest when it's appropriate to wear them. Each chapter is organized roughly from the general to the specific, beginning with a short introduction. From there we proceed to the best basics for your wardrobe and build, and from there to short how-tos on specific styles, fabrics, and materials. Each chapter concludes with pointers about storing and caring for your clothes once you have them, because investing in quality also means investing in longevity.

Of course, it doesn't matter how polished the individual items in your wardrobe are if you can't pull them into a coherent, signature look. One way to develop sartorial aplomb is by looking at how style icons, past and present, did it. You'll see a lot of them in these pages. We're calling them "The Originals": Cab Calloway, Cary Grant, Miles Davis, Marlon Brando, André 3000, Idris Elba. These are men who turn almost any combination of clothes, from the simplest white T-shirt and five-pocket jeans to the most sophisticated Savile Row suit, into a striking, but hardly ever ostentatious, personal statement.

What all these illustrious guys have in common is taste. Not boring, I-followed-the-rules "good" taste, but risky, I-tossed-the-rules-I-didn't-like taste. Which, in the end, is the only taste that counts: informed, fearless, unapologetic, personal. Don't think it was always an easy matter for the sharp dressers we've chosen; often, they got to look so cool only by giving their attire a lot of careful thought.

Case in point: Frank Sinatra, the scrawny kid from Hoboken turned Palm Springs dandy, took as much professional pride in his appearance as he did in his recordings, continually refining both until his look and his sound seemed effortless. Sinatra gave instructions to the centimeter on the length of his collar points and the break in his trousers. He made stylishness appear both manly and easy. Even Marlon Brando, the poster boy for couldn't-give-a-damn insouciance, developed enough cocky sartorial smarts to know that his T-shirts and black-leather motorcycle jackets were more flattering on him than expensive tailoring would be. (The famous torn T-shirt that Stanley Kowalski wears in *A Streetcar Named Desire* was Brando's rehearsal garb.)

The great style icons are inspirational in two senses: They show us how to pull off a truly personal look and why it's a worthwhile goal in the first place. Dressing well is a way of integrating and expressing your personality. It's a way of finding out about yourself and expressing that knowledge to the world at large. It may not be as complex or revelatory as painting or writing a book, but it's an honest, meaningful method of distinguishing yourself from the pack. And when you're heading out on your own, it's always best to carry a map.

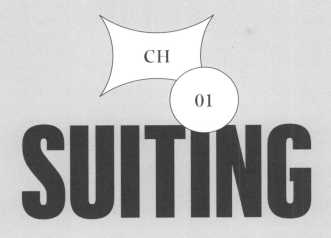

CH

01

SUITING

Since it was introduced in the nineteenth century, the modern suit has been at the apex of personal style. If you doubt us, try this simple experiment. Some evening, go to a nice hotel bar, where you don't know anyone, wearing jeans and a T-shirt.

CONTINUED

The jeans don't even have to have holes in them, and the T-shirt can be clean. Now, return to the same bar the next evening wearing a nice suit. Take note of the difference in the reactions of the bartender and of the other patrons in the bar. Remember them. Write them down if you must.

You see how a sleek, well-cut suit can turn an everyman into the ideal man: serious, powerful, physically charismatic. For this we thank Beau Brummell, the legendary Regency-era arbiter of fashion who turned his back on the flamboyantly beribboned menswear of the previous centuries and instead embraced perfectly tailored, neutrally colored pieces in luxury fabrics, like linen and chamois leather. Brummell became the talk of the town for his sartorial derring-do (and for the unheard-of habit of bathing daily), but his MO works as well today as it did two hundred years ago: good taste and style are best expressed by an impeccably tailored, elegant suit.

Brummell's renegade approach was bolstered by the neoclassical revival, which reintroduced the masculine physical ideal: the Greek athlete, with a torso in the shape of an inverted triangle. Deft English tailors transformed the plain wool coat, waistcoat, and breeches of the country gentleman into an elegantly molded, comfortable urban garment that gave its wearer what appeared to be the physique of a classical sculpture. It didn't take long for the middle class to figure out that what the suit did for the landed gentry it could do for them, and once democratizing ready-to-wear garments were introduced in the mid-nineteenth century, would-be fine gentlemen emerged everywhere.

At the beginning of the twentieth century, Neapolitan tailors, impressed by the high-style Edwardian clothing of vacationing British nobs, mastered the tricks of the London suit-making trade. But they modified the construction techniques to produce a supple, weightless, unlined jacket that is relaxed and comfortable in Naples's hot climate. Giorgio

Armani successfully adapted the loose-jointed Neapolitan suit in the 1970s. He gave it a fuller cut and a distinctive Milanese slouch that dominated the stylish man's wardrobe for the next decade, famously appearing on Richard Gere in *American Gigolo* in 1980.

The Armani look was a more sophisticated version of the American "sack" suit. Introduced around the turn of the twentieth century, the shapeless suit soon became the universal business uniform and, mass-produced in gray flannel, the very symbol of white-collar conformity. A favorite of Ivy Leaguers and midlevel corporate strivers during the Eisenhower era, its hegemony was challenged by the relatively snappy navy blue two-button suits of President John F. Kennedy and by the slim-blade, dark-and-narrow ensembles worn by the cast of the 1960 film *Ocean's Eleven*. The Rat Pack suit was called the Continental look, and it originated in Rome; it's what the disaffected charmers wear in the movies of Fellini and Antonioni.

Since no one has yet devised a plausible replacement for formal male dress, the only way to fight the suit's lingering aura of conventionality has been to play obsessively with its fabric, details, and silhouette. A fitted jacket with slim trousers that just barely graze the top of your wing tips was the default for nearly two decades—and that's still a great move. But lately, the pendulum has been swinging toward a more expansive view of how a suit should look. Relaxed fits, oversized blazers, and wide trousers, along with an irreverent attitude toward getting suited itself, have all become part of the style conversation. The lines between elevated and the everyday have been blurred, and so thankfully there's no longer one "right" way to wear a suit.

THE ANATOMY OF
THE PERFECT SUIT

THE ONLY ONE YOU NEED FOR WORK, WEDDINGS, FUNERALS, PARTIES, AND EVERYTHING IN BETWEEN

NATURAL SHOULDER

Keep it fairly natural—too much padding makes the suit look like it's wearing you.

NOTCHED LAPEL

Your lapel speaks volumes. A small, high notch right on the collarbone is traditionally the mark of a killer suit, a minor detail that makes your off-the-peg suit look closer to classic bespoke.

DEEP NAVY, WOOL CLOTH

It's dark enough to appear professional but also lighter and classier than rather dour black. Lightweight wool stands up best to repeated wearing and can be worn year-round. An interesting texture like hopsack, or even a small-scale herringbone weave, lends some subtle depth to an otherwise simple suit.

FITTED WAIST

Unless you're embracing a baggier look, the jacket should be somewhat fitted at the waist, to give your body a more dynamic shape.

SIMPLICITY

The more streamlined the details, the more widely you will be able to wear this suit. Avoid extra pockets and flamboyant stitch detailing for this go-to basic.

TROUSERS

Flat-front trousers are considered cleaner, but pleats are a stylish swerve. A cuff's added weight keeps your pant creases sharper. A cuff should be between one and a half and one and three-quarters inches in height.

THE TERMS: JACKETOLOGY

Six obscure bits of suit jargon you may never need to use but might be glad to know all the same.

THE DROP: The term used to denote a suit's shape–e.g., a "drop six" means a trouser waist six inches smaller than the chest.

THE JIGGER: The single button in a double-breasted jacket that is always kept fastened.

BOSOM POCKET: Pockets cut into the suit's fabric, usually covered with a flap.

TICKET POCKET: The third pocket above the side pocket of a jacket (normally the right one), usually with a flap.

KISSING BUTTONS: How cuff buttons on expensive suits are sewn so they almost overlap up the sleeve.

THE SCYE: The term for the armhole, the size and shape of which often determine the jacket's fit.

THE DEFINITIVE STYLE RULES
NAVY SUITS

1. A navy suit can be worn with both black and brown belts and shoes. A black suit cannot.

2. If you're wearing a tie, tuck in your shirt (and even if you're not, consider tucking).

3. Three things you need in that shirt underneath your navy suit: comfortable fabric, a collar type that matches your tie, and quality pearl buttons. One thing you don't: cuff links.

4. Navy doesn't have to mean plain. Instead of toying with loud stripes, try a textured fabric like herringbone to give your navy suit added character.

5. Two expensive suits in your wardrobe are better than five cheap ones. One of the two should be navy.

6. Know your neck size. You should be able to fit one finger between your collar and your neck when your shirt is fully buttoned.

The RULES

NAVY IS THE MOST FLEXIBLE SUIT COLOR YOU CAN BUY.

Followed closely by charcoal and medium gray.

THE NAVY SUIT
FOUR DIFFERENT WAYS

You won't find anything more versatile, more worth the investment, than a great navy suit. It's the utility infielder of a man's closet, keeping you sharp whether you're eyeing a spot at the bar or a seat on the board. Think classic two-button, with a subtle texture and a tailored fit. The jacket can also work as a free agent paired with other pants in your closet, because the secret to a flexible wardrobe is wearing clothes of such undeniable quality that they'll work in any scenario. And a good navy suit will do just that.

FOR SUNDAY AFTERNOON

A lightweight sweater underneath the jacket, matched with a pair of corduroy pants, keeps things casual but sharp.

FOR MONDAY MORNING

Sure, you've got to button up for the boss and a client meeting, but bold stripes preserve your individuality.

FOR THURSDAY NIGHT

The shirt's subtle yet colorful stripes and high, thick collar make it the perfect party shirt to complement the suit's fitted silhouette.

FOR FRIDAYS

A classic three-button, with a subtle texture and a tailored fit. Ditch the pants and pair the jacket with khakis, corduroys, or a pair of dark jeans.

THE FOUR ESSENTIAL SUITS

THE BASICS YOU NEED, IN THE ORDER YOU NEED IT.

THE STAPLE

Start with navy blue (see page 32). It's formal enough for all manner of buttoned-up business, and it's much classier than black.

THE SPARE

Add some variety with a light-gray suit, and opt for a lightweight worsted wool rather than wintry flannel.

THE PINSTRIPE

Ease your way into patterns with a fine pinstripe. It's always in style, and as a bonus for those short of height (if not stature), the vertical lines make you look taller.

THE BOLDER CHECK

Now for some fun. Get creative with patterns like this classic glen plaid; it adds texture and depth to your closet.

16

PEE-WEE HERMAN AND THE SHRUNKEN SUIT

It seems it's always the weirdos who push the boundaries of style. Shrink-wrapped in his gray polyester suit, Pee-wee Herman was a beguiling blend of the nerdish and the knowing, a spiffily dressed man-child who refused to grow up. Who knew that the trim-fitting, ankle-bearing style of the guy who spoke to armchairs would be strutting down New York runways twenty years later? People snickered when designer **Thom Browne** launched his signature gray flannel suit, with its Pee-wee-like proportions, but as the new chairman of the Council of Fashion Designers of America and the head of a $500 million label, he too is getting the last laugh.

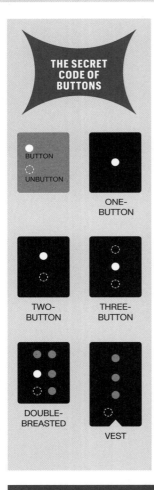

THE SECRET CODE OF BUTTONS

BUTTON
UNBUTTON

ONE-BUTTON

TWO-BUTTON

THREE-BUTTON

DOUBLE-BREASTED

VEST

BUTTONS AND YOU
A HANDY GUIDE

THE SHORT GUY

Lengthen your silhouette by choosing a one-button jacket with natural shoulders. The deep V will give length to your torso.

THE SKINNY GUY

A double-breasted jacket gives more width to a slim torso. The button stance and the extra cloth add bulk.

THE BROAD GUY

A two-button jacket gives a slimming effect similar to a one-button jacket, with a deep V between the lapels to lengthen the torso.

THE BIG AND TALL GUY

A three-roll-two suit—in which the top button "rolls" under the lapel and only the center button is fastened—offers a slightly shorter V without looking dated. Its fit should be close and comfortable.

The RULES

IT'S WORTH NOTING THAT YOU SHOULD TAKE ANY LIST OF HARD RULES WITH A BIG GRAIN OF SALT . . .

. . . including this one.

18

THE MATH ON THE DOUBLE-BREASTED SUIT

THE THREE TYPES OF CLASSIC DOUBLE-BREASTED JACKETS ARE DETERMINED BY THE NUMBER OF BUTTONS.

THE SIX-ON-ONE

Six buttons, of which only the bottom-right button is functional. This style, popularized by the Duke of Kent in the 1930s, has a long, rolled lapel and a wider, lower gorge that exposes more of the shirt and tie. Some people think this creates a longer line that's flattering on shorter men.

THE SIX-ON-TWO

Six buttons, of which only the center and bottom-right buttons are functional. Only the center button is used; the lowest button is always left undone. Although this is the most traditional of double-breasted styles, its high, tight gorge looks crisp and modern.

THE SIX-ON-SIX

Six buttons, of which all three buttons on the left are functional. All buttons are usually done up, creating a very high, tight gorge. A rather military or naval style, it's most often found in traditional blazers with metal buttons; in suits, it floats in and out with the fashion tide.

THE FOUR-ON-ONE

Four buttons, of which only the bottom-right button is functional. Because the button stance is higher on the jacket than a six-button configuration, the gorge normally lies somewhere between the lower six-on-one and the higher six-on-two.

The ORIGINALS

AL CAPONE AND THE PINSTRIPE SUIT

When Prohibition turned gangsters into businessmen and Al Capone adopted the suit traditionally worn by bankers (who were considered upstanding citizens), little did he know that one day he'd be trading pinstripes for jail stripes. The exaggerated stripes, shoulders, and lapels that Capone favored gave the suit a wiseguy aura it has never totally shaken. Still, in restrained form, the pinstripe is fit for a president. On a savvy actor like **Yahya Abdul-Mateen II**, it's co-opting the symbol of boardroom privilege to show that this is what success looks like too.

THE NINE PATTERNS YOU SHOULD KNOW

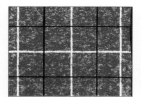

1. WINDOWPANE

Good for: Business suits that moonlight as party wear.

2. HOUNDSTOOTH

Good for: Bold jackets and suits for special occasions.

3. CHALK-STRIPE

Good for: Hearty cold-weather suits that mean business.

4. PINSTRIPE

Good for: Business of any kind.

5. BIRD'S EYE

Good for: Cocktail suits that get noticed.

6. HERRINGBONE

Good for: Casual blazers and cold-weather trousers.

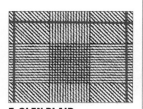

7. GLEN PLAID

Good for: Classic suits for the office.

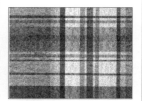

8. MADRAS

Good for: Warm-weather blazers paired with jeans.

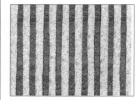

9. SEERSUCKER

Good for: Suits and pants that look sharp in torrid heat.

JACKETS AND PATTERNS: A FIELD GUIDE
BECAUSE YOU CANNOT SURVIVE ON SOLID COLORS ALONE.

PATTERNED TIE, STRIPED SHIRT

This pairing looks best with plain jackets or mélange flannels.

STRIPED TIE, STRIPED SHIRT

The tie's stripes should always be bolder than the shirt's.

CHECKED SHIRT, STRIPED JACKET

The shirt's checks should be as big in scale as the jacket's stripes.

CHECKED JACKET, KNIT TIE

Match a visual texture (a check) with a tactile texture (knitted silk).

STRIPED JACKET, STRIPED SHIRT

The shirt's stripes should always appear bolder than the suit's.

BOLD-CHECK JACKET, PLAIN SHIRT

The bolder the check, the plainer the shirt.

PATTERNED JACKET, STRIPED SHIRT

Contrast the shirt's stripes with a fine-patterned suit.

FLANNEL JACKET, CHECKED SHIRT

The bolder the shirt check, the plainer the suit cloth.

The RULES

A WARDROBE REQUIRES ONLY TWO BLAZERS:

The navy two-button blazer is the most functional—it can be dressed up with a tie or down with jeans. The lightweight tweed works for the weekend or any event where there's a chance of having a conversation about the films of David Lynch.

The CLASSICS

THE TWEED SPORT COAT

Before Gore-Tex, before Polartec and microfleece, there was . . . the tweed sport coat? Robust and hard wearing, tweed's popularity grew out of the English obsession with Scotland that reached a mania in the mid-1800s with Queen Victoria and her husband, Prince Albert, who bought Balmoral Castle there and traveled to Scotland as often as possible. Wealthy new industrialists from the south began buying up castles and land from impoverished Scottish owners for the newly popular sports of grouse shooting and deerstalking, for which tweed was the requisite uniform. Tweed was also the fabric of choice for the upper-echelon Englishmen who founded the Alpine Club in 1857. They wore tweed sport coats—most notably Norfolk jackets, with numerous pockets to hold all their climbing gadgets—and tweed breeches. In America the tweed sport coat came to symbolize the WASP in all his Ivy League splendor and then became a semaphore for all-purpose bookishness (think Wes Anderson). But the professorial uniform need not look fusty: worn with stylish twill jeans or a bold striped shirt, it's a solid anchor of good taste, plus plenty of streetwear-influenced brands are breathing new life into tweed with designs that are a far cry from what hung in your grandfather's closet.

THE THREE JACKET SHOULDERS

NATURAL
It looks like: The Roman Empire—a gradual, stately decline. *Why you should wear it:* Shows off, rather than hides, your body shape. Tailors prefer it.

ROPED
It looks like: The top of the sleeve is laid over a piece of rope. (It isn't.) *Why you should wear it:* Conveys a rigorous formality and a little old-school glamour.

PADDED
It looks like: You're a comedian from the 1980s. *Why you should wear it:* You're slight and could use more implied lateral bulk.

TOM WOLFE AND THE WHITE SUIT

Like fellow Southern clotheshorse Mark Twain, author Tom Wolfe made the white suit his signature look in a dramatic urban wardrobe. His first white suit, purchased one summer in the early 1960s upon his arrival in New York, conferred instant personality on the relatively unknown Wolfe. No one since has pulled off the white suit so successfully, that is until **Shawn Mendes** showed up to the VMAs in a billowy white suit that would have had Wolfe and Twain fanning themselves and exclaiming, "My! My! My!"

THE FORGOTTEN SEASON
THE SUMMER SUIT MANUAL

Maybe it's because we're used to stretching that wool suit we spent so much money on last fall as far as it can possibly go, but summer somehow falls by the sartorial wayside. It's doomed to be the forgotten season. But it shouldn't be, because there are options. Cases in point: lightweight combinations like these. The light colors and breathable fabrics are made especially for hot July afternoons. So are unconstructed, or "Neapolitan," jackets, which do away with all the padding and canvassing that trap heat. They are your friends, so take advantage of them.

LINEN

Linen is the perfect summer suiting fabric, thanks to its light weight and open weave, which makes it naturally breathable. The inevitable wrinkles also lend it a more relaxed vibe, so try losing the tie or just wearing a tee underneath.

SEERSUCKER

To avoid looking like a dandy, you can dress a seersucker suit down and make it more modern by wearing it with a light-colored linen sweater.

CHINO

The same material found in your favorite pants also works as an excellent summer suiting fabric, since its cotton fibers and light weight will keep you comfortable in the sun. Opt for classic khaki (as Barack Obama infamously did) or choose a bold, seasonal hue.

ALL IT TAKES ARE A FEW SIMPLE OUTFITS. AND THERE'S ONE SECRET—THE SIMPLER THE BETTER.
—*Cary Grant*

THE MYSTERIES OF
SUMMER
DRESSING—SOLVED

WHICH COLOR IS LEAST SUITED TO SUMMER?
Black is cool, but sweating bullets isn't. Try light gray, khaki, or a brighter shade of blue as alternatives.

WHY SHOULD I WEAR WOOL IN THE SUMMER?
Ask any desert dweller: The most comfortable fabric in extreme hot or cold is wool, which regulates body temperature. Look for high-twist or "fresco" wool, which allows for a very open weave that air can pass through easily, letting you feel every breeze. Bonus: the naturally "bouncy" nature of high-twist wool makes it extra wrinkle resistant.

WHAT'S THE DEAL WITH THE SEERSUCKER SUIT, AND WHAT DO I WEAR WITH IT?

Defined by its lightweight, puckered fabric (which allows for greater air circulation on your skin, therefore keeping you cool in warm weather) and commonly striped appearance, the seersucker suit is a staple that your closet needs. You can dress it down with a graphic tee and white sneakers and dress it up with a light button-down and some dress shoes.

BUT IS IT OKAY TO NOT WEAR SOCKS IN THE SUMMER?
Sure. Just remember that those no-show socks provide the same look but without the odor.

SPEAKING OF SHOES, WHAT SORT MIGHT I WEAR WITH A CREAM OR IVORY SUIT?
A pair of natural-leather wing tips will lessen the heady snazz of the suit and draw on its classic Southern-gentleman style.

HOW DID THE SUMMER SUIT GET ITS START?
With the New Deal, which gave men more cash to spend on the forgotten season.

ANY DRESSING DON'TS I NEED TO KNOW ABOUT?
It's tempting, but don't just roll with your heavy winter suit and shoes. The somber tones will look out of place, but you'll also pay for it—in perspiration. Also, while producer, rapper, and designer Pharrell Williams looks amazing in a short suit, be realistic about whether you do.

HAND SIGNALS
WHAT TO DO WITH YOUR HANDS WHEN YOU'RE DRESSED FOR BUSINESS

To look as if you actually belong in your top-of-the-line suit, it's not sufficient just to buy the suit and put it on with care. Those are merely levels one and two. To sell yourself convincingly in an expensive suit, you need to know what to do with your body, particularly your hands, when you're in it. These gestures are the secret to looking great in fine tailoring. Here are three easy moves to try at your next social occasion. Each will have you looking as if you're wearing the suit instead of the other way around.

THE KING CHARLES
THE MOVE: Absent-minded fiddling with the cuff links.
THE PURPOSE: To ensure that precisely one inch of your shirt's cuff is showing at all times.
THE BONUS:
With your arms balanced, your suit's fitted shape is emphasized. You'll look royal.
WHEN IT'S DONE: Transitional movements—between the limo and the official reception, in elevators, or arriving at parties.
PITFALL: Do not attempt this if your shirt does not have French cuffs. You'll look nervous.

THE SPREAD AND TUCK
THE MOVE: With your jacket unbuttoned, use both hands to push back the sides, allowing you to slide your hands into their respective front pant pockets.
THE PURPOSE: To give your hands something to do when making small talk.
WHEN IT'S DONE: At wedding receptions, awaiting your turn at a bar, and before the start of an event.
PITFALLS: It's okay to let one side go, to leave a hand free to shake someone else's or to grab a drink. But as soon as that hand has nothing to do, be sure to retuck.

THE UPPER EAST THUMB
THE MOVE: One hand sitting in the side jacket pocket with your thumb jutting forward.
THE PURPOSE: To appear at ease even in stuffy surroundings.
THE BONUS: The crook of your arm away from your body is slimming.
WHEN IT'S DONE: At yacht clubs and ritzy East Coast cocktail parties.
PITFALLS: Do not put undue weight on your pocket edge. The hand should float while inside the pocket. Also, never do this with both hands at once. Symmetry, in this case, is a no-no.

The RULES

JACKET SLEEVES ARE TAILORED SO THAT HALF AN INCH OF SHIRT CUFF SHOWS WHEN YOUR ARMS ARE AT YOUR SIDES.
This does not make your sleeves look shorter. It makes your arms look longer. Work it out.

27

THE INVITATION TRANSLATOR
DECIPHER THE DRESS CODE

WHAT IT SAYS	WHAT IT IMPLIES	WHAT IT REALLY MEANS
Black tie	Tuxedo only, and not a black suit	Tuxedo only, and not a black suit
Cocktail attire	A "fun" suit	In general, *cocktail* means darker colors, but you can experiment with colors other than blue and gray. And you still need to wear a collared shirt.
Black-tie optional	You can choose between black tie and a suit	The wedding party will be wearing formal; you may join them—or not
Semiformal	Black tie, but with a twist	You're not wearing a tux, but you are wearing a suit and tie
Dressy casual	Shorts and sneakers are acceptable	Nope, shorts and sneakers are still not acceptable, even if they're "dressy" shorts and sneakers
Casual	You know, whatever	Casual at a wedding does not mean the same thing as casual on your own time
Nonstandard	Wear your bunny suit	Lean on the hosts to give you some sort of guidance here, or go dressier

David Beckham in a linen suit, a great option for dressy casual dress codes

THE ANATOMY OF
THE TUXEDO

YOU DON'T NEED ALL THE BELLS AND WHISTLES, BUT YOU DO NEED A TUX AND A HANDFUL OF THE RIGHT ACCESSORIES FOR WHEN EVENING WEAR IS REQUIRED.

1. THE WHITE SHIRT

White piqué cotton, bib front or with vertical razor pleats, pressed until it's immaculate. French cuffs are essential, as are studs, unless you go ultra-sleek and opt for a fully covered placket. A turndown collar is more comfortable; a wing collar is more dressy.

2. THE TUX

Peaked lapels, single- or double-breasted. Notched lapels make you look like a waiter. Black wool barathea is classic, but a lighter plain weave is better for summer comfort. Grosgrain lapels last longer; satin has a habit of snagging and showing its age quicker. Midnight blue is very cool. And leave your wallet at home and take a money clip instead, which won't distort the lines of your tux.

3. THE BOW TIE

Silk satin or silk grosgrain, black. Adjustable versions make tying easier, but you should tie it yourself.

4. THE POCKET SQUARE

White, in cotton or linen, not silk, which will slip.

5. THE CUMMERBUND

The cummerbund (from the Hindi word for "waistband"), anachronistic or not, is still essential. Without it, you look as if you're not trying.

6. THE SHOES

You do not need patent-leather shoes, although they look sharp. A good pair of well-polished cap-toe oxfords will suffice.

31

HOW TO BUY A BUSINESS SUIT

The jacket's shoulder pads are supposed to sit on your shoulder. If they droop off and leave dents in the cloth, the jacket is too big. Go down a size.

The jacket's sleeves should never reach farther than the point where the base of the thumb meets the wrist. If they do, go down a size.

You do not need enough room in your jacket to house a family of raccoons. Go down two sizes.

Pants should touch the shoes with only an inch of cloth to spare. Anything more should be taken up.

1. PRIORITIZE.
The basic unit of workplace style is the navy blue suit. It should be your first purchase. After that comes solid charcoal gray. Then striped and checked versions of these two fundamental shades.

2. SPEND. WISELY.
It's about quality, not quantity. Instead of two just-OK suits, spend the same amount on one truly great suit and get it tailored by a professional.

3. MITIGATE HEADACHES.
Sure, the weightless vicuña blends and the fine-as-silk Super 180's look good. But they're also a pain to take care of. All-season, midweight cloths feel good summer through winter, and resilient weaves like hopsack and gabardine won't wrinkle on a red-eye.

4. MAXIMIZE UTILITY.
Chosen carefully, the three basic suits— one navy, one gray, and a pattern—can constitute an entire wardrobe. A dozen shirts and ties, in different colors and fabrics, turn them into a limitless backdrop for creativity.

5. CHECK THE FIT.
While suit fits have come a long way since the days of slim only, a perfectly fitted business suit still means high armholes, a slight silhouette at the torso, and nothing too baggy at the crotch. You owe it to yourself to discover and revel in the power of a perfect fit.

HOW TO CHECK THE FIT

THE TROUSER BOTTOM

You've got two options: break or no break. For the former, ask your tailor for a one-inch break in your front crease. The hem of your pants should cover most of the tied laces and slope slightly downward toward the heel, stopping about an inch above the sole. The front crease of your trouser leg should "break" slightly at midshin. For the latter, the crease should be dead straight, only grazing or not touching your shoes at all.

THE SHOULDER AND THE LAPEL

How your jacket fits at the shoulder is the first sign of whether you know your size. Look for higher, smaller armholes and a narrower sleeve. It fits properly if there's no overhang at the shoulder pad or, conversely, your shoulder does not bulge out at the top of the sleeve. A smooth curving line should fall from sleeve head to cuff. No outline of your own shoulder should appear in the sleeve, and the sleeve's head should never sag.

THE WAIST

The correct waist measurement is not at your hips, as you've been trained to believe, or your belly button. It's halfway in between. While Your correct waist measurement may cause initial shock if you've been using the wrong numbers all along, but knowing it will make your suit fit better. There should be no creases or ripples radiating from the single fastened button. If there are, switch up a size.

THE SHIRT CUFF

A quarter to a half inch of shirt cuff should always be visible. Maintaining this is one of life's greatest challenges. And the sleeve should rest a half inch below your wristbone

THE COLLAR

The collar of your jacket should sit well on the shoulders and not buckle or pucker or stand away from or conceal your shirt collar. A half inch of shirt collar should be visible at the back.

THE JACKET LENGTH

The bottom hem should be level with your knuckles. (Alternatively, it should be just long enough to cover your rear.)

WHICH SHAPE ARE YOU?

THERE'S A SUIT TO FIT EACH ONE.

Suits are often, and unfairly, maligned as a uniform of the corporate class, the dress code of the office drone. Walking through any large city's financial district during lunchtime might confirm this bias, but nothing could be further from the truth. The suit is, in fact, an infinitely customizable garment capable of being tweaked to fit any situation, and in the hands of a professional, any person, regardless of shape or size. Here's how to find yours.

YOUR SHAPE: SQUARE

Your jacket should be just long enough to cover your rear end but not cut too much on the long side; that only shortens those efficient legs. Go for a two-button with a double vent, which gives the illusion of longer legs. Opt for dark, striped cloths, with no wide shoulders or lapels.

YOUR SHAPE: THE INVERTED V

One- and two-button jackets with a deep gorge, or opening, will elongate the body. Narrow pinstripes and chalk stripes also do the trick. Balance your waistline with strong shoulders and wider lapels.

YOUR SHAPE: TALL AND THIN

Create breadth by adopting a double-breasted suit. Draw attention to the chest and neck by way of brighter hues and patterns on your neckties and shirts. Do not be tempted to widen yourself with excess padding, though; you'll look even skinnier.

YOUR SHAPE: THE ATHLETIC V

A two-button suit gives a deeper gorge and allows room for bigger biceps. Look for larger armholes and wider sleeves. Your guns should not be visible through cloth. Found the ideal jacket but the pants are too big? Grease the sales clerk into switching out the pants for ones from a smaller suit.

THE RIGHT SUIT AMPLIFIES YOUR PHYSICAL STRENGTHS AND DIMINISHES YOUR SHORTCOMINGS

A larger person should wear solids, especially dark ones, and avoid large, loud patterns. A short person elongates their silhouette with a suit, particularly a striped suit, eschewing the sport-coat-and-pants look because it chops in half what little verticality he has. And ye of the ample booty: Go with ventless jackets or those with a rear vent rather than side-vented models, which flap above your prodigious glutes like a signal flag.

HOW TO BUY FOR YOUR BODY TYPE

YOU ARE	YOU WANT	AVOID
BIG & TALL **(E.G., SHAQUILLE O'NEAL)**	Pants with cuffs to break up your seemingly endless inseam; pants with slimming, shallow pleats; a dark navy suit.	Anything with horizontal lines, which accentuate your girth; anything with vertical lines, which make you look even taller.
LONG & LEAN **(E.G., BARACK OBAMA)**	Anything with horizontal lines to help you look broader; double-breasted jackets add heft and breadth.	Anything with vertical lines, which make you look even taller; overly tight suits and jackets that advertise your thin limbs.
SHORT & STOCKY **(E.G., DANNY DEVITO)**	Single-button suits that have a deep V at the chest to make the torso look longer; V-neck sweaters that do the same.	Anything with horizontal stripes or busy plaids, which break up the body's vertical lines; a deep trouser break, which visually shortens the legs.
SHORT & LEAN **(E.G., TOM CRUISE)**	Two-button suit jackets that work in proportion to your torso; thicker fabrics (like corduroy), which offer the illusion of heft.	Anything baggy or loose, which draws attention to your size.

WHY IT'S MADE THE WAY IT'S MADE

WHY SHOULD I HAVE WORKING BUTTONS ON MY SLEEVE?

If you're going to get a great suit, then pay the extra eighty-five dollars for buttonholes. Trust us. Hand-sewn buttonholes are still a sign of a good suit, but be aware that even cheap suits have mock buttonholes, sewn by machine.

MY SUITS ALWAYS SEEM TO FORM A BUMP AT THE BACK OF MY NECK. IS THIS NORMAL?

Normal, no. Common, yes. The bump happens when there's too much fabric above the shoulder line, causing it to pucker. A tailor should be able to fix this, because nowhere on your suit should there appear anything that might be called a pucker. Yes, even if the suit was on sale. The jacket should hug your neck gently and rest cleanly and comfortably on your shoulders. No bumps.

WHY IS AN UNLINED SUIT MORE EXPENSIVE THAN A LINED ONE?

When there's no lining, any visible seams must be perfectly finished; there's no room for error. It's painstaking and costly, but the jacket will be softer and cooler. Our choice is the partially lined jacket (like the one turned inside-out, above); pieces of viscose cloth sewn in strategic places make it easy to slide the jacket on and off without compromising the cool fabric.

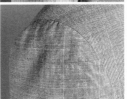

DO I NEED SHOULDER PADDING IN MY SUIT?

Personal preference. Suits generally have a soft shoulder (fabric only) or a structured one (varying amounts of padding). Either is appropriate, but the soft shoulder is cooler, looks more casual, and lets the fabric drape more naturally. The structured shoulder, slightly padded, will look more crisp and add to your stature. Beware, though, of too much padding, which will make you look like you came from the '80s.

The RULES

THERE IS NO ALTERING OF SHOULDERS.

If the jacket doesn't fit there, it never will.

THE HIDDEN DETAIL
FUSED VS. CANVASED

Inside every proper suit jacket, between the exterior cloth and the lining, lies the secret of its shape: a layer of cloth called the canvas. A bespoke suit or a top-end ready-to-wear design features what's known as a full-hand canvas, sewn into the jacket by hand, stitch by stitch, so that it echoes the curves of the chest, gives the lapel its roll, and in a sense, determines the very integrity of the jacket. Cheaper brands, however, use a process called fusing, in which a synthetic interlining is heated by machine until it adheres to the exterior fabric and provides the jacket with its rudimentary shape. Until you're caught in a rainstorm, that is, when the glue dissolves, leaving blisters on the chest and lapels. Although fusing has long been deemed inferior to hand canvasing, this is no longer universally so. Improvements in fusing technology have made it possible to create fused suits that fit better than some canvased ones. But never offer this opinion to a tailor, unless he be of robust constitution.

HOW TO TELL

Pinch an inch of the jacket's fabric, preferably between the bottom two buttonholes. If you feel only two layers, that means the jacket is fused: You will feel only the exterior and the inner facing. If you feel three layers, that means the jacket is canvased, and what you're sensing is the facing, the exterior, and the canvas itself floating in between. If after performing this test you're still not sure, ask the salesman. If he doesn't know what you're talking about, you're probably in the wrong store.

SUIT SEAMS

Hand-sewn seams are composed of a single thread running through the fabric in a wavelike pattern. When done properly, they are smooth and pucker-free and are more resilient to creasing and stretching than machined seams.

Machine-sewn seams are composed of two threads looped tightly around each other in a chain-like pattern. They are sturdy, but the loops create puckers in the fabric, which can worsen over time as the fabric stretches.

RULES FOR BUYING A SUIT

1. There's a reason it's on sale. When in doubt, go with the two-button.

2. Beware the sales clerk who works on commission.

3. No two suit brands are cut the same way. So if you don't get a good fit from one brand, try a different one.

4. Listen to your tailor, but always follow your gut.

5. Re: your gut—a good tailor can help you with that.

6. The more elaborate the pattern, the less often you'll wear it.

7. Assuming you won't set off alarms, take your prospective purchase outside and look at it in daylight. Hidden depths and colors may appear.

8. Most reputable shops offer on-site tailoring services. Take advantage of them.

9. Order a suit online only if you're familiar with the brand's fit or you've checked the return policy (or both).

10. A three-piece suit says you mean business; in fact, it says you mean to take over the business.

WHAT TO EXPECT WHEN YOU BUY A BESPOKE SUIT

A bespoke suit can be a man's greatest gift to himself, and the term *bespoke* even has its origins on Savile Row, London's tailoring mecca. (When a customer chose a bolt of fabric for his suit, that fabric would then "be spoken for.") Yet the sheer scope of options, from cloth and cut to lapels and lining, can be daunting. How do you avoid a minor existential crisis?

First, find a good tailor. The best way is to ask a man you trust; if a suit maker has the respect of your peers, he probably deserves it.

The infinite variety: A good tailor will guide you through the maze of choices with your wits intact. And a clever tailor will always advise that your first suit remain free of any showy details (the better to appreciate the fit and quality of work.)

The process: The tailor will take up to twenty-five measurements before sending you on your way. You'll return for the first fitting, when every square inch of the embryonic suit is evaluated and adjusted. The suit will go through two or three further cycles over several weeks. Finally, slip on the finished product and smile.

Wait time: Six weeks to a year

Cost: In the $3,000 range

Number of fittings: At least three

HOW TO
KEEP A SUIT FOREVER

THE BRISTLED CLEANING DEVICE

Your great-grandfather used a suit brush. He was a wise man. Far from being a pointless tool in the age of dry cleaning, the clothes brush (along with steaming) lets you put off dry cleaning. Before brushing, air out your suit near an open window, then lay it flat on a table.

THE RAIN DEFLECTOR

These days even high-end designers use cheaper and less-labor-intensive fused linings to give jackets the structure they need. When your suit jacket gets wet, it puckers and becomes misshapen. No amount of pressing can bring a suit back from this condition.

THE GARMENT-SUSPENSION DEVICE

Every time you don't store your jacket on one of these (it's a hanger, by the way), you're cutting its life. Look for the same qualities in hangers as you do in your best pirate friends: a generous thickness to the shoulder and a strong metal hook. A suit hanger should be broad and shaped enough to support a jacket the way it might hang on you. Anything less and it risks looking like it has just been slept in.

THE STEAM-DELIVERY TOOL

You need to dry-clean a suit only once a year. Any more and the process can weaken the suit and ruin its shape. Steaming is the ideal solution for keeping the suit looking immaculate. Avoid areas with multiple layers, like the chest and lapel, as steam can shrink delicate fabric and potentially melt fused linings. Instead, focus on wrinkle-prone spots like the arms, waist, and back.

HOW TO STORE A SUIT

OUT OF SEASON: Dry-clean the suit first to ensure against moth damage. Take time to lay it flat (to reduce creases) before the next step. Fully seal it in a suit-length or hanging Space Bag (see page 206), and remove the air with a vacuum cleaner. Hang on a well-shaped hanger.

IN SEASON: On a generously shaped hanger in a zipped-up suit bag.

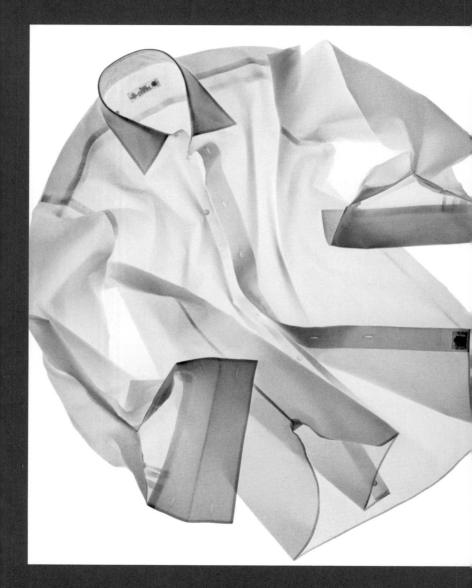

SHIRTING AND KNITWEAR

CH

02

They're the one-two punch of everyone's closet, thanks to their timeless versatility. So while they may not need an introduction, there are a few facts, and more than a few tips, you should know about this dynamic duo.

CONTINUED

41

For much of the nineteenth century and the Edwardian era leading up to the Great War, traditional dress shirts had detachable white linen collars, starched rigid and worn high. A writer for *The Gentlemen's Journal* complained in a 1909 article about "the curious, stiff, high, turn-over, close-locking collars which I see in hotel corridors and streets. How hideous they are." Right. We've all been there, man.

The demobilized servicemen returning home from the front were apparently also in no mood for restrictive civilian clothes. In the manner of impetuous young people everywhere—whether the Lost Generation or Generation X, Y, or Z—gentlemen of the Jazz Age embraced change. Their sartorial rebellion was expressed in the form of fine shirts that draped naturally over the body, with soft collars that folded back from the neck. F. Scott Fitzgerald paid homage to the new style in *The Great Gatsby*, when Daisy Buchanan buried her face in a pile of Jay Gatsby's luscious-hued English shirts and sobbed uncontrollably at their overwhelming beauty.

Men ever since have enjoyed choosing from an astonishing array of style options. Roaring Twenties collar styles, including the button-down, the tab, the pinned, and the Barrymore, have continued to go in and out of fashion. The Windsor, an extreme spread style designed to accommodate the hefty tie knots favored by the eponymous Duke, made its debut in the 1930s. It's still the dressiest of dress-shirt collars, sported by corporate moguls and deposed royals; beyond it, you're in tuxedo territory—the only social situation in which you're still obliged to wear a white shirt.

And what is there to say about this minimalist wardrobe staple? For starters, there is no dressy occasion when wearing a white dress shirt is a faux pas. It always looks good, provided that it's clean, it fits you, it has all its buttons intact, and it has met an iron at some point in its recent history. True, it can seem an unadventurous choice, particularly with a business suit, but there is no shame in embodying a fine tradition. Worn with jeans and a sport jacket, a crisp white shirt is as dashing a statement as ever.

The sport shirt—an open-collar, short-sleeve, button-front style in woven or knitted fabrics—first showed up in the 1930s too, mostly at exclusive winter watering holes in Monte Carlo and Palm Beach, since only the rich needed smart leisure clothes during the Depression. These new shirts, made of light cottons and linens, were intended to be worn without a tie but still look casually elegant. Their twenty-first-century descendants have a slightly vintage feel that captures the timeless cool of the postwar era. (Think: Palm Springs and Cary Grant, circa 1959.)

Not all the sport shirt's progeny are so pedigreed. That great social leveler, the T-shirt, started life as humble underwear but, made of tissue-weight cashmere or silk, can now carry a three-figure price tag. Somewhere in between lies the perfect tee: high-quality, 100 percent cotton, crewneck, black or white, true to its American roots. Worn with a well-cut pair of chinos, a belt, and loafers, it will take you pretty much anywhere.

The wool sweater has proved even more universally popular. Originally the garb of laborers, farm workers, and fishermen, it was adopted enthusiastically by Jazz Age urbanites, for whom slipping on a stretchy pullover had the same liberating charge as throwing out starched collars and shirts. In England, the actor and playwright Noël Coward, fed up with collars and ties, began wearing colored turtlenecks, "actually more for comfort than for effect," he said. "Soon I was informed by my evening paper that I had started a fashion." No generation since has been willing to give up the comfort and ease of the sweater, and for our money, there's no more comfortable and better-looking option than a merino wool or cashmere V-neck worn with a tie and a sport jacket or suit. Because it comes in myriad guises—including contemporary zip-fronts and bold colors—changing your style can be as simple as slipping on a different pullover.

THE ANATOMY OF
THE DRESS SHIRT

EVERYTHING YOU NEED TO KNOW TO BUILD THE PERFECT SHIRT WARDROBE

THE BOTTOM BUTTON

On the well-made dress shirt, the buttonholes are all cut and sewn vertically into the placket (see below), except for the bottom one, which is horizontal. This is because shirts used to button into the front of the trousers to prevent blousing. Even though pants no longer accommodate this, the finest shirtmakers have clung to the tradition.

THE BOX PLEAT

A nice detail on the back of a dress shirt is the box pleat, which drops from the yoke (the piece of fabric that goes over the shoulder) to the bottom of the shirt and provides more room to move.

THE HAND-SEWN SHOULDER

Only on a very high-quality (read: expensive) dress shirt will the sleeve be handsewn to the yoke with the stripes of each piece lining up perfectly.

THE CONTRASTING COLLAR

Created so that white-collar types could wear colorful shirts without losing status, the contrast collar is rarer these days but hasn't disappeared. Shown is a collar cut on the bias to withstand many washings without shrinking.

THE PLACKET

The place where the buttonholes run down the front of your shirt is called the placket. On a well-made dress shirt, the placket is a separate piece of material (left), sewn on with a single-needle machine. Alternatively, in super-lightweight summer dress shirts, there may be no placket at all (right), in order to keep the shirt cool and elegant.

THE GUSSET

A gusset is added for reinforcement at the bottom of the shirt where the front and back join.

THE BUTTONS

Mother-of-pearl buttons are a sign of a well-made shirt. The thicker the better, to withstand washings; four holes mean a better bind.

**EVERY MAN
NEEDS A WHITE
DRESS SHIRT**

On the hierarchy of necessity, a white dress shirt sits somewhere between a belt and a toothbrush. Can you imagine not owning one? But merely owning any white dress shirt is not enough. The perfect specimen must:

· Fit exquisitely
· Have thick buttons (preferably mother-of-pearl)
· Be constructed of fine cotton
· Be of impeccable quality (the simplicity of the shirt will reveal any imperfections)

Wear your perfect white dress shirt with something striking—like a dark suit and tie and a white pocket square—and everyone notices. Everyone. Words like *sharp, dapper,* and *fantastic* are suddenly showered upon you. Even friends and colleagues who are typically stingy with compliments will go out of their way to tell you you look great. The look is nothing new. But worn right, it works like a charm.

**YOUR COLLAR SHOULD
COMPLEMENT YOUR FACE**

Round face? Point collar.

Narrow face? Spread collar.

Oval face? Congrats, genetics allows you to wear whatever color you like!

THE CLASSICS
THE BROOKS BROTHERS BUTTON-DOWN

The term *button-down* is often misused by fashion rookies to describe a shirt that has buttons down the center from top to bottom. No. The term actually refers to having the ends of the shirt collar fastened to the shirt by buttons. John Brooks, grandson of the founder of America's most venerable clothing brand, did not invent the button-down shirt, but he made it a pillar of American style. At a polo match in England in 1896, Brooks noticed that players had added buttons to their shirt collars to keep them from flapping while riding. He immediately adopted the technique. Seeing its usefulness, he brought the practice to America and began selling the classic button-down dress shirt in 1900. It defined America's knack for a more casual, functional approach to dressing well, and by the 1920s it was a stateside staple. The button-down has survived in fashionable and square wardrobes alike, despite its conservative connotations.

The ORIGINALS

ANDY WARHOL AND THE DRESS SHIRT

"Why do people think artists are so special?" Andy Warhol once quipped. "It's just another job." Warhol felt art was a business just like any other. As if to prove the point, he often wore components of a businessman's uniform—a button-down dress shirt and necktie—straight up and without irony. His ensemble meant exactly what it implied: I'm a commercial artist; what of it? If surface truth was the only kind Warhol believed in, he wore the truth on his sleeve. For **Stanley Tucci,** the truth is likely found at the bottom of a perfectly cooked bowl of cacio e pepe. The actor turned food influencer keeps us dreaming of Italy, and keeps us thinking about his crisply pressed button-ups.

FREQUENTLY ASKED QUESTIONS

CAN YOU WEAR A BLUE SHIRT WITH A WHITE COLLAR, OFTEN CALLED A BANKER'S SHIRT, WITHOUT A TIE?

Short answer: no, wear the tie. Most men who wear the contrasting collar are interested neither in comfort nor in expressing their individuality. If you're trying to break free of your own gray-flannel prison, try something that's meant to be dressed down, like a sweatshirt.

WHEN DO I NEED TO TUCK IN MY SHIRT?

For some, the only answer to this question is "always." For others, a few kinds of shirts can be worn untucked with impunity. These include a casual shirt with a bottom hem that cuts straight across and doesn't hang below the hipbone, anything knitted (e.g., polo shirts), and of course fitted T-shirts. These days, a good rule of thumb is: The more formal the environment, the more reason you have to tuck.

A FIELD GUIDE TO THE SHIRT

THE CUFF

1. THE ONE-BUTTON BARREL

Here's your basic anywhere, anytime cuff. Functional and modern, with none of the fiddliness of cuff links, the one-button cuff is right for normal office days but not too dressy.

2. TWO-BUTTON NOTCHED BARREL

A nice detail that, for formality, is just short of French. The notch and slightly longer cuff upgrade an everyday suit and can dress up a sport coat worn with trousers or jeans.

3. THE FRENCH

Still the most dressed-up choice, the double, or French, cuff is best for showing a quarter inch of shirt cuff from underneath your jacket sleeve. With a simple silk knot or a plain silver cuff link, it shows them that you know exactly what you're doing.

THE COLLAR

1. THE BUTTON-DOWN

The least formal of collar styles. Traditionalists say you shouldn't wear it with a suit; rule breakers of a particularly American ilk will disagree.

2. THE MEDIUM SPREAD

A handsome option appropriate with almost any suit and face shape and with a variety of tie knots.

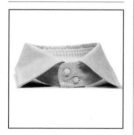

3. THE TWO-BUTTON SPREAD

Set on a wider band with two buttons at the neck, the tall collar can be worn without a tie altogether, since it's substantial enough on its own. Sits nice and high on the neck, so it works well for the tall, wiry guy who needs some height to cover the neck. Its tie knot: the half Windsor.

4. THE STRAIGHT POINT

A classic shape that works for all ages and neck shapes. Good for the round-faced or short-necked man, since it neither accentuates girth nor hides the neck. Its tie knot: the four-in-hand, which goes with everything. Don't forget the collar stays (those plastic or metal spears that keep your collars from sagging).

THE FABRIC

You know there's a whole range of weaves, even before color plays into it. But did you know that certain weaves beg pairing with certain ties? Now you do. There are many options, so here are some of the most popular.

1. SEA-ISLAND COTTON
This very light, almost translucent woven cotton works best with knitted silks and other lightweights, such as linen ties.

2. DIAGONAL-WEAVE BRUSHED TWILL
A textured cotton with a fine pattern, this meaty weave can carry off the chunkiest of woven silk ties.

3. END-ON-END BROADCLOTH
Combines white with another color cotton in a very fine weave that results in a tiny check. May be paired with sturdy fabrics like thick silk wovens.

4. PIMA
This lightweight, supersoft option coordinates with lightweight silk, cotton, and linen ties.

THE RULES OF WEARING SHIRTS

HOW TIGHT TO KNOT YOUR TIE, WHEN YOUR SHIRT COLLAR IS JUST RIGHT, AND MORE

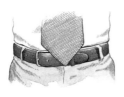

TIP AT THE WAIST

The tie's point should just touch the waistband of your suit trousers, assuming, of course, that your waistband is properly on or just above your hipbone.

DIMPLE IN THE MIDDLE

Just one dimple. In the middle, secured with a pinch. Edges that are curled forward are sloppy. Practice until it's right.

TIE IT TIGHT

When tied, the knot should sit high under the collar, so that practically no material can be seen above the knot between the collar edges. Any tighter and you risk discomfort.

THE TIE CLIP

Designed to keep your tie in place, the tie clip should slide in from the wearer's right to grip both the tie and the placket of your shirt around the middle of the sternum.

KNOW YOUR NECK SIZE

The collar fits when you can just slip your index and middle fingers side by side snugly between your collar and neck.

STICK LETTERS HERE

Place a monogram anywhere you like. The most classic location is directly below the middle of the breast pocket. Visible but not obtrusive.

AN OVERSIMPLIFIED GUIDE TO
MIXING PATTERNS
HOW TO PAIR SHIRTS AND TIES WITHOUT INCIDENT OR INJURY

1. FINE-STRIPED SHIRT

Best bet: A textured knit tie.

2. CHECKERED SHIRT

Best bet: A dark solid tie with a subtle pattern.

3. WINDOWPANE SHIRT

Best bet: A patterned tie that echoes the color of the check.

4. GLEN-PLAID SHIRT

Best bet: A thick-striped tie that accents the bolder plaid.

5. WOVEN SHIRT

Best bet: A dark tie with stripes that match the shirt.

6. BENGAL-STRIPED SHIRT

Best bet: A dark solid tie with a slightly less subtle pattern.

51

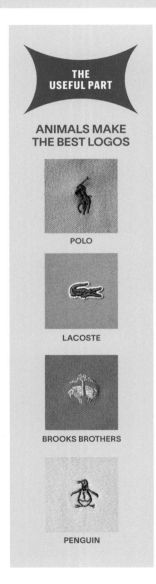

THE USEFUL PART

ANIMALS MAKE THE BEST LOGOS

POLO

LACOSTE

BROOKS BROTHERS

PENGUIN

The CLASSICS

THE POLO SHIRT

Inspired by the wool-knit jerseys worn by polo players since the 1890s, René Lacoste appeared at the 1926 US Open in a short-sleeved, soft-collared, white cotton pullover. Custom-made polo shirts were soon indispensable sportswear items for members of the leisure class on both sides of the Atlantic. In 1933, Lacoste and the French knitwear manufacturer André Gillier began marketing cotton piqué shirts embossed with the now-familiar alligator logo—a branding innovation that launched an ark's worth of miniature animals nestled on sporting chests. Lacoste's alligator, introduced to the American market in 1952, was joined by Munsingwear's penguin in 1955 and Ralph Lauren's polo player and pony in 1972. A casual wear perennial that, like blue jeans, can be dressed up or down, the polo shirt became something of a fashion item in the prep-obsessed early 1980s (never mind that fuchsia pink and flipped-up collars might not have been what the estimable M. Lacoste had in mind).

The ORIGINALS

RENÉ LACOSTE AND THE POLO SHIRT

Legendary French tennis champ René Lacoste didn't pick up a racket until he was fifteen, but his tenacity on the court earned him the nickname Le Crocodile. His determination extended to his attire: In 1926, he debuted the white polo shirt on court, disregarding the regulation dress code that included a long-sleeved, stiff-collared shirt, tie, and long white flannel pants. Half a century later, the chameleonic polo lent ironic cool to art-rock superstars like **David Byrne** of Talking Heads, who often wore one onstage.

The ORIGINALS

MIILES DAVIS AND THE TURTLENECK

In 1954, a young Miles Davis—eyes closed and lips pursed—nonchalantly plays the trumpet while seated, wearing a turtleneck. If you were expecting him in his Ivy League–influenced green Oxford shirt or his '80s Issey Miyake looks, don't worry: One of the many gifts of Davis's career is that he wasn't afraid to change with the times, his music or his style. But in the mid-'50s, Davis in a laid-back turtleneck is the epitome of jazz's quiet cool. Speaking of quiet, actor **Alexander Skarsgård** isn't someone we normally associate with sartorial risk taking, but when he paired a copper colored merino turtleneck with a blue-green suit, we knew the turtleneck has found its next innovator.

The CLASSICS

THE CABLE-KNIT SWEATER

First emerging as a wardrobe staple in the United States during the 1950s, the cable-knit became a favorite of ski instructors who, as Esquire noted, "were exerting a tremendous influence on skiwear." Long before then, though, the cable-knit sweater was crafted for the fishermen of the rugged Aran Islands off the west coast of Ireland. The yarn is woven to create an effect of crisscrossing ropes. The cable pattern represented their fishing ropes and was believed to be a charm for good fortune at sea. Each fisherman's family had its own stitching, similar to a family crest, and it has been said that the fishermen knew, should they go overboard, that they could be identified by their sweaters alone. These days, though, the cable-knit works just as easily on dry land with a nice pair of jeans and suede boots.

The RULES

EVERY PERSON LOOKS GOOD IN A BLACK TURTLENECK SWEATER.. Buy one. Wear it.

ALBERT EINSTEIN AND THE V-NECK SWEATER

The world of academia may not be the first place to look for forward-thinking style, but many an intellectual has his own dress code based on comfort and simplicity. When Albert Einstein pulled a classic V-neck sweater over an open-collar shirt in the 1940s, little did he know he'd be making sartorial history with a utilitarian (let's call it rumpled) ensemble that still looks relatively modern. Costume designers soon calculated that putting a star in a V-neck sweater—Ryan Gosling and **Donald Glover** included—conveyed instant smarts.

HOW TO WEAR A SWEATER TO THE OFFICE

"Casual Fridays" are now every day at most workplaces. That means the suit and sport jacket have fallen by the wayside, but you still need a smart way to look professional while feeling comfortable. Enter the sweater. Whether it's a V-neck, a crewneck, a zip-front, or a cardigan, the sweater can easily sub in for a jacket, especially if it's high quality—linen or fine-gauge cotton in summer, merino wool or cashmere in winter—and never misshapen or showing signs of wear. To keep the look dressed up instead of down, pair with classics like well-cut trousers, a great leather belt, and loafers.

THE V-NECK

You can't go wrong with a fine wool or cashmere V-neck worn with good wool trousers. Extra credit: a bright contrasting tie and a striped shirt. Dress down with cords or jeans.

THE POLO

Filled with '70s swagger, the polo sweater is having a bit of a moment right now, and it comes in several varieties: short-sleeve or long, patterned or solid, pullover or button-front. Try it with menswear's other darling of the moment, pleated pants, to complete the vintage look.

THE ZIP-FRONT

A fine-gauge zip-front sweater adds warmth with style. Leave the neck open to show off your shirt and tie. For a dose of Italian sprezzatura, look for beautiful detailing, like a color lining or a contrast collar.

The RULES

IF YOU CAN'T PUT YOUR ARMS ALL THE WAY DOWN AT YOUR SIDES . . .
. . . then your sweater is way too thick.

HOW TO BUY CASHMERE

Lots of things bill themselves as "pure cashmere," but there's a reason some cashmere sweaters cost $90 and others cost ten times as much. The best variety comes from Mongolia and northern China and is called long staple cashmere, meaning the individual fibers measure at least 1.4 inches in length. (Rule number one: The longer the fiber, the better the fabric.) These strands can be twisted into especially strong, featherlight yarns, and the subsequent dyeing, weaving, and finishing processes are precisely monitored to ensure quality. Manufacturers pay upwards of $100 per kilogram for the good stuff—barely enough to make a single suit jacket.

Due to rising demand, it's now common to find bales of "pure cashmere" that contain a percentage of far cheaper lamb's wool; some of these lesser blends are coated with an emulsion that imparts the soft hand of top-quality cashmere but also gives the fabric a greasy residue. (Rule number two: Rub your fingers together after handling your prospective purchase to check for said residue.) Unfortunately, there's no universal manufacturer's symbol for high-quality cashmere, but most high-end brands have staked a reputation on carrying only the real thing.

Sure, the prices are high, but that leads to our third and final rule: You get what you pay for.

A REMARKABLY DETAILED GUIDE TO IRONING A SHIRT

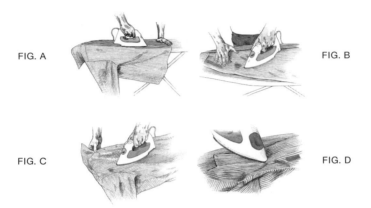

FIG. A

FIG. B

FIG. C

FIG. D

1. START WITH THE BACK of the unbuttoned shirt flat on the board and the sleeves hanging down both sides of the rounded end. Press using gentle circular motions. Use steam if needed (usually it's best if the shirt is not bone-dry, especially with cotton). Work away from the center to the side seams. { FIG. A }

2. SELECT A SLEEVE, placing the underarm seam straight along the board and nearest to you. Smooth it out, holding it tight and flat while you firmly press the seam itself. Work away from the seam, being careful to sharpen any pleats. Repeat with the other sleeve. { FIG. B }

3. MOVE ON TO THE CUFFS, opening them completely faceup (the side with the button on it). Iron from the sleeve edge of the cuff, working out toward the ends and sides of the cuff. { FIG. C }

4. OPEN DOUBLE CUFFS completely, and

work in the same way. Press a sharp fold in the cuff only after you have pressed it open. Do not press the folded-back cuff flat. The only crease should be the one around the very end of the cuff.

5. MOVE ON TO THE FRONT of the shirt, laying each side flat and smoothing it out. Work around the buttons, taking care to press the plackets (the strips where buttons and buttonholes are placed) on both sides firmly. Work away from the plackets toward the side seams. { FIG. C }

6. OPEN THE COLLAR faceup and lay it fully flat. Working from the outside edge of the collar, use tiny circular movements to avoid creasing the cotton against the stitching on the edge of the collar, which would be obvious and unsightly. Keep the iron pointed toward the shirt label. Fold the collar down, and press in the top ridge firmly with your fingers. { FIG. D }

AN ILLUSTRATED GUIDE TO
FOLDING

THE T-SHIRT	THE SWEATER	A STACK OF SHIRTS

1. Lay shirt faceup. Pinch shoulder with your left hand and chest with your right.

1. Lay sweater facedown with arms spread. Smooth out any wrinkles.

1. Stack shirts faceup on top of one another, with arms spread.

2. Crossing left hand over right, pinch the shoulder and the bottom hem together.

2. Touch the left sleeve to the bottom of the right hem.

2. Fold the bottom half of the stack under the top half.

3. Lift the shirt, uncross your hands, and pull the shirt taut. Shake it, and fold over.

3. Touch the right sleeve to the bottom of the left hem, making a neat rectangle.

3. Place one set of sleeves across the chest, and fold the other across it.

4. Lay the shirt down faceup, and smooth and straighten accordingly.

4. Fold the top half over the lower half, and straighten accordingly.

4. Place shirts directly in suitcase. Remove upon arrival, and hang in closet.

60

SEW A BUTTON

1. Make a single stitch in the shirt only, about ⅛-inch long. Leave a 3-inch end of loose thread.

2. Do the same again, but this time perpendicular to the last stitch to make a cross.

3. Thread the needle up through one hole in the button and down through the diagonally opposite hole. Hold the button about ⅛ inch away from the shirt throughout. Next time use the other holes. Repeat four times.

4. Wrap the thread tightly around the shank that has been created between the button and the cloth to create a tight pillar.

5. Push the needle through this pillar a couple of times. Cut the thread close to the pillar.

To launder your own shirts, machine wash them in lukewarm water with a nonbleach detergent. Hang them to dry near but not on a radiator, a window, or another source of heat. Steam or iron them when they're almost dry. If you prefer to have them professionally cleaned, look for a laundering option rather than dry cleaning to extend their life span. Shoddy dry cleaning can ruin a dress shirt. The process can damage the fibers and can give whites a yellow tint. When laundering, specify that your shirts should be hand ironed and with no starch, which adds to the deterioration of your shirts and is never completely removed when washed. A lot of cleaners don't offer hand ironing, so you might need to shop around.

PANTS AND DENIM

Could anyone have predicted that denim "waist overalls," first made in 1873 by Levi Strauss & Company to outfit prospectors in the California gold rush, would become the most influential—and profitable—garment ever invented in America?

→
CONTINUED

Considering that during the first half of the twentieth century, few men would have found jeans acceptable wear for anything other than manual labor—and we're not talking raking the sand trap or rolling the tennis court. It's hard to believe now, with jeans being the default for pretty much everything except weddings and funerals, but even in the dog days of summer, a relaxed outfit prior to the First World War might have consisted of a dark suit jacket worn with flannel or linen trousers.

But postwar, the youth-conscious society demanded a new ease and informality in dress. There were speakeasies, violent workers' strikes, and unemployment lines—who needed fancy, restrictive suits? Even E.E. Cummings didn't object when publishers started lowercasing his name. Clearly, conventions of all sorts—sartorial included—were under siege. So came the need for more casual, stand-alone trousers that could be worn variously with blazers, sport jackets, shirts, and sweaters. Wool, both tropical weave in summer and flannel in winter, proved the most popular fabric for dressy sport trousers: In addition to retaining its shape well, wool is an efficient insulator in the cold, heat, and damp. Initially restricted to gray and white, it was soon available in a range of colors, though the most vivid hues were generally reserved for resort wear—except by the future Duke of Windsor, who often shocked the old guard with his brightly colored apparel.

Even in class-conscious England, the privileged were snipping away at rigid dress codes, with trousers sending some powerful signals. Fashionable young men in the mid-1920s were switching overnight from slim, elegantly cut flannels to Oxford bags—enormously wide pleated trousers made popular by students at the eponymous university. British intellectuals were also adopting corduroy for town use in an effort to show solidarity with the farmhands who wore it to do real work. The humble, cut-pile cloth got the royal seal of approval when the Duke began to favor it, and corduroy has been a class-bending trouser ever since.

Although blue jeans have never entirely lost their original sweat-of-the- brow utilitarianism, they gained cachet with city dwellers as part of a fad for the romanticized Old West in the 1920s and 1930s. After the Second World War, the urban middle class began to adopt the sturdy, copper-riveted pants as leisure wear; movie idols like Marlon Brando and James Dean did the same, and the rest is history (see page 77). As the Woodstock era faded, denim jeans began to lose their counterculture cool—but not their market share: Almost everybody everywhere, including Jimmy Carter and Ronald Reagan, had at least one pair of inexpensive dungarees, which became increasingly acceptable in all sorts of social and business situations. Andy Warhol even wore them with a tuxedo jacket to the White House in 1985 because, he said, "jeans are so easy."

Then, in the late 1970s, jeans became "designer," as brands such as Gloria Vanderbilt, Fiorucci, and Calvin Klein successfully chased disco kids and denim dollars. Those designers did the early legwork for a new category of luxury pants, "premium" jeans, which appeared at the millennium's dawn. These high-end niche labels justify their elevated prices by producing limited-edition styles in high-quality fabric, often using artisanal production methods. Today the term *denim head* denotes a hobby just as acceptable and commonplace as *gearhead* once was.

James Dean also helped popularize America's other major contribution to men's below-the-belt sportswear: the casual cotton trousers known as khakis and chinos. Both names reflect the pants' military origins (see page 72). Like jeans, khakis are comfortable, accessible, and easy to care for, but they carry a more imposing set of associations than does working-class denim. Perhaps that's why, paired with a sport coat, button-down shirt, and loafers, even threadbare khakis appear upright and proper; combined with a cashmere sweater, sea-island cotton dress shirt, and elegant slip-ons, well-cut chinos look like a million bucks.

THE ANATOMY OF
THE TROUSER
WHAT TO LOOK FOR IN THE PERFECT PAIR OF PANTS

THE FRENCH FLY

The nifty tab-and-button closure distinguishes a high-quality pair of trousers from your everyday variety. The zipper is attached to an extended waistband, which takes stress off the zipper and ensures that the front lies flat.

LINED WAISTBAND

The waistband is lined to maintain its shape. Options include a split seam and a V-notch in the back so the trouser can be altered for a perfect fit.

TAPED SEAMS

Seams are pressed, with their edges taped or piped for reinforcement and to keep them lying flat.

LINING WHERE IT COUNTS

Good-quality trousers are lined through the crotch and often to just above the knees; the extra fabric ensures durability and plain old comfort.

CUFFED VS. UNCUFFED

Cuffs add weight and draw attention to the line of the pants. If you're on the short side, forgo the cuffs. Cuffed trousers should have a straight hem; an uncuffed hem should be longer in back, hitting the lower heel.

PLEATS (OR NOT)

Most trousers—even when they come with a suit—are flat fronted, thanks to two decades of slim fit's dominance. But the pendulum has been swinging back to pleats over the last few years, which is cause for celebration (see page 68).

A GUIDE TO
TROUSER TYPES

Sometime in the past decade, pleated pants got a bad rap. Someone, somewhere convinced the world that flat-front trousers were the ne plus ultra for modern men, whereas pleats were what Grandpa used to hide his beer belly. Pleats, however, have a lot going for them, particularly in the roominess department. Granted, they do nothing to tighten up your silhouette, but for a lot of us, our silhouettes weren't all that tight in the first place.

FLAT FRONT

More or less obligatory when it comes to modern suits. Optional details like slash or welted pockets vary the minimal look.

REVERSE PLEATS

The pleats fold inward, producing near flat-front trousers. The most common pleated style of the past few years.

REGULAR PLEATS

The pleats fold outward. Double pleats are seen more and more these days but single are still the go-to.

The ORIGINALS

CAB CALLOWAY AND PLEATED PANTS

In the 1930s, a style of suiting known as the "English drape"—boxier shoulders, roomier armholes, and flared pants—was popularized by the Duke of Windsor. But Black tailors in Harlem took the less restrictive style to voluminous new heights by exaggerating the proportions. Dubbed "drapes" (you probably know them as zoot suits), the style was popularized by jazz singer Cab Calloway, whose appearance in the 1943 musical *Stormy Weather* cemented the look of big, pleated pants as a fashionable protest (that same year, Mexican youths in LA were violently attacked for wearing the look). Today designers mass and niche are experimenting again with volume in pants, with some very wide results. Today, designers both mass and niche are experimenting again with volume in pants, like Steven Stokey-Daley whose heavily pleated trousers have been worn by none other than **Harry Styles.**

THE ANATOMY OF
CHINOS

NO ARGUMENTS, GENTLEMEN: THEY'RE ONE OF AMERICA'S GREATEST CONTRIBUTIONS TO THE WORLD OF STYLE. HERE'S WHAT MAKES THEM RIGHT.

THE COLOR

Khaki is a color. Chinos are a pair of pants. Know the difference but feel free to use the terms interchangeably.

RELAXED FIT

With noticeably wider legs and no sign of a crease, relaxed-fit pants look loose and athletic and may even have some fraying at the cuffs.

THE CRUMPLE FACTOR

Some light wrinkling and a slouchy construction typify the most casual breed of chino. Wash them only when absolutely necessary. Creases are just another way of saying your chinos have been ironed. They also imply that you iron your socks (see Chinos Fact #2, right).

POCKETS

The best chinos have four pockets. Anything more or less and you're asking for trouble.

PLEATS AND CUFFS

Both can add formality, as does a tab closure at the waist, but plenty of more casual styles offer them now too. Cuffs can range from a slight turn up of the bottom hem to a chunky roll, and pleats come in single, double, and—for the fashion forward—triple. The beauty of chinos is that it's all up to you.

THE MOST UNDERRATED PANTS

Despite its salt-of-the-earth connotations, America's official trouser has its nuances.

CHINOS FACT #1

If the roll looks like you're wearing a bagel around your shins, you've rolled too much.

CHINOS FACT #2

A crease down the front of a pair of khakis adds fifteen years to the age of the wearer.

CHINOS FACT #3

Think of your chinos as a leather briefcase. That first scar will break your heart, but you'll learn that they are at their lived-in best just before they disintegrate.

CHINOS FACT #4

Unless you're on safari, limit the number of khaki items in your outfit to one. Better yet, apply this rule even while on safari.

CHINOS FACT #5

Chinos are the most comfortable pants to sleep in. Keep this in mind if you're going drinking with a friend who loves shots.

The ORIGINALS

GEORGE CLOONEY AND CHINOS

George Clooney certainly is not the first movie star to wear chinos, but he pulls off the look so effortlessly— with a black T-shirt, leather lace-ups, and no socks—that it's as though he reinvented casual cool (movie-star good looks and an athletic build don't hurt). The military origins of chinos may lend a tactical quality to these classic pants, but on Clooney they're a world away from the starchy military style of **Douglas MacArthur and his fellow generals.**

THE ANATOMY OF JEANS

A CELEBRATION OF HISTORY'S MOST ENDURING PAIR OF TROUSERS

THE FIFTH POCKET
Jeans just don't look right without a coin pocket—even if you've never used it (and never will).

COPPER RIVETS
First patented in 1873 by dry goods merchant Levi Strauss and Jacob Davis (a tailor who was a customer of Strauss's), rivets originally reinforced pockets and extended the life of the pants. Today they remain on most brands, part of the DNA of jeans.

BUTTON FLY
Though the button fly can be a pain—especially with stiff jeans—it's the best way to pay homage to denim's hard-laboring heritage.

WASH AND DISTRESSING
This is retail industry speak for how worn your pair looks, even if they still have the tags on. There are many levels to how washed and distressed your pair can be. Our advice? Don't take it too far, whether it's with rips or fading (you're better off creating those yourself, naturally, with wear).

LEG SHAPE
Narrow or baggy, tapered or straight, the lower leg defines what shoes you can wear. And with jeans you can wear pretty much anything.

The ORIGINALS

THE RAMONES AND DENIM'S LO-FI APPEAL

Up against a weathered, graffiti-strewn wall stands Joey, Johnny, Dee Dee, and Tommy, stone-faced in their black leather jackets and Levi's 505 jeans. If there ever was an advertisement for the punk rock attitude and aesthetic, Roberta Bayley's image of the Ramones for their 1976 eponymous debut is it. Slim but not skinny, distressed but not destroyed, their denim look would set the template for how rockers should dress for the next thirty-plus years. Don't believe us? Look up any image of **the Strokes.**

HOW TO WEAR PANTS
OR, THE PROPER LENGTH AT WHICH TO WEAR THEM

It is a constant debate, really. How far down on the shoe should the pant leg extend? There is, of course, a right and a wrong ankle altitude to which a man should extend the bottom of his trousers. Too long and you look sloppy. Too short and it looks like you're wearing capri pants. To help you out, here's our handy guide on how to wear your pants, the cuff edition. Take it with you to the tailor, or take a photo with your phone for reference.

CUFFED SUIT PANTS	UNCUFFED SUIT PANTS	CHINOS	JEANS
The weight of the cuff (1.5 to 1.75 inches wide—anything more looks like you thought about it too much) straightens the trouser leg and gives it a clean line. The hem should not slope.	If you're more conservative, opt for a slight break in the front crease that gently slopes to a slightly longer back hem. For a more contemporary look, let the hem just graze the top of your shoes (aka no break).	Current tastes dictate one of three paths: pooled at the ankle (you're under twenty-five), cuffed (you're a creative director), or cropped (you follow street-style accounts).	See: Chinos
The golden rule			
Nothing ruins the look of a smart suit as quickly as dumpy shoes.	Whatever you do, make sure the socks match your pants color. And don't be the "wacky socks" guy.	They're just chinos, don't overthink it.	Denim looks best with sneakers, boots, or loafers. A shoe that's slim and elegant, with a thin sole and a pointy toe, won't cut it.

The CLASSICS

LEVI'S

You could say it all started in the seventeenth century in the town of Nîmes, France, where a durable cloth was being woven called serge de Nîmes (denim, get it?). But the famous story of Levi's began in San Francisco, where tailor Jacob Davis made a pair of work pants with copper rivets to strengthen the pocket corners. In 1873, Davis, along with Levi Strauss, a German-born cloth merchant who supplied Davis with his fabric, pieced together sixty-eight dollars to patent the riveted work pants. The 501 label was added in 1890; the famous red pocket tab, in 1936. And the double line of stitching on each back pocket is one of the oldest surviving trademarks in clothing.

In the 1950s and 1960s, thanks to powerfully attractive, Levi's-sporting movie rebels like Marlon Brando and James Dean, jeans and a T-shirt or leather jacket became the uniform of the emerging youth culture. In 2003 the world's oldest pair of Levi's was purchased by Levi Strauss & Co. for its archive. Originally woven in a New Hampshire mill, the denim dates to the 1880s. These days, Levi's is a multibillion-dollar brand with its own football stadium and stores around the world, but it's still the first name in American denim.

5 TIPS FOR WHEN YOU BUY DENIM

1. The heaviest acceptable weight for denim is about fourteen ounces per square yard, although modern denim can go as light as seven ounces per square yard. Below seven ounces, you might as well opt for chambray.

2. The two measurements you need when buying denim are waist and inseam, in that order. Your inseam is measured from crotch to anklebone. Your waist is either your true waist for high-rise styles or your hips for mid-rise styles. And for low-rise jeans? Run in the other direction.

3. Always say no to embellishments.

4. Never use a dress belt with jeans. Wear one with some heft or Western flair, the kind that looks like it could cope with actual work.

5. Things like acid wash and baggy-fit denim once fell out of fashion's favor, but they've recently have returned. Still, you can never go wrong with a straight-leg pair in a mid-blue wash.

THE SAVILE ROW FOLD

Need to stop your suit trousers from falling off their hangers? Try the Savile Row fold, perfected over generations by the staff at London's finest custom-tailoring emporiums.

1. Start with the trousers upside down and straddling a hanger.

2. Fold one leg in through the hanger, dropping the bottom hem in between until it sits just above the crotch.

3. Fold the second trouser leg over the first and through the hanger. Shake the hanger. Nothing happens. Clever, isn't it?

. . . AND OTHER IDEAS FOR HANGING PANTS

The ideal hangers for pants are the sort with two spring-loaded slats of wood that grip the hem of the trousers so that they hang upside down. This allows creases and side hems to strengthen under gravitational pull.

The RULES

GRAY FLANNEL PANTS ARE THE NAVY BLAZER OF COLD-WEATHER TROUSERS.

They go as well with a T-shirt as with a white Oxford and tie, so you might want to stock up.

LET THE SOCKS MATCH THE PANTS, NOT THE SHOES.

EYEWEAR
Looks bad. Feels bad. Just plain bad.

INK PEN
Especially not on a plane.

BULGING KEY CHAIN
And lose the mini bottle-opener.

A FEW WORDS ON SHORTS

Forget opening day at the ballpark or last-minute meetings with your accountant—the surest sign that spring has arrived is kneecaps as far as the eye can see, with people breaking out their shorts and settling in for a few months of barelegged recklessness.

Not too long, not too short, and hitting just above the knee. For most guys, this is the ideal short length. That being said, short inseams have been creeping up as of late to a vintage-inspired 5-inch length, which isn't as scary as it sounds. But whatever you do, don't wear really long ones, since those are not, in fact, shorts but short pants. There's a big difference. Huge.

And there's the question of patterns. A simple pair of solid color chino shorts can't be beat, which is why you should have multiples, but life's too short not to experiment a little. That used to mean patterns like madras (see page 21) or embroidered critters, both of which look dated, and like a Cape Cod cliche, at this point. Opt instead for stripes, graphic patterns, or some camo.

FREQUENTLY ASKED QUESTIONS

WHAT'S THE RULE FOR SWEATPANTS NOW? CAN I REALLY WEAR THEM ANYWHERE?
The humble sweatpant had one of the greatest runs of all time over the past decade. First, the slim jogger rehabbed its slovenly rep, and then COVID lockdown sent sales skyrocketing. But that's all in the past now, so what's a cozy boy to do? For starters, head to page 148 to learn more about the various types of sweatpants you need these days. Then keep in mind that while high-end Italian luxury purveyors like Canali and Brunello Cucinelli make sweatpants now, it still doesn't mean you can wear them to an in-person client meeting or dinner with your in-laws. No matter how swaggy, no matter how technical they've become, they're still not a substitute for "hard pants" (sorry).

FOOTWEAR

Shoes are often considered the foundation of any outfit because even the most expensive, well-tailored suit will be ruined by the wrong footwear (politicians, we're talking about you). Thankfully, it's not hard to build said foundation with just a few versatile pairs.

→
CONTINUED

The next time you're in your office, take a look at everyone's feet. Unless you work at a white-shoe firm, you're probably going to see sneakers—lots of sneakers—including on your own feet. For the sake of comfort and personal style, that's great. But despite what sneakerheads might tell you, man cannot live on trainers alone. "Hard bottoms" still have a place in your rotation; they just share equal, uh, footing with your athletic-inspired pairs.

Never mind sports—it was the exertions of military men, rather than athletes, that historically influenced men's footwear. In the early nineteenth century, the well-dressed man wore high boots in both town and country. Two popular styles, the Wellington and the blucher, were named respectively after the British and Prussian field marshals—joint victors at Waterloo—who devised them. Wellington had his London shoemaker design a soft, close-fitting calfskin boot that was tough enough for battle yet sufficiently elegant for evening wear. It remained fashionable until the 1870s but was immortalized as the "Wellie," a rubber farm boot introduced in France more than 150 years ago. The blucher was an ankle boot that laced in front over a tongue. The field marshal specified it for his troops because it was easy to get on and off; with the invention of metal eyelets in the 1820s, lacing and unlacing it became an even simpler and quicker matter.

During the early twentieth century, the oxford, whose many variants include the cap toe, the wing tip, the brogue, and the balmoral, was the quintessential and most successful gentleman's shoe, and it persists today as the workingman's classic. The British dominated the world market for men's fine footwear between the world wars, which meant a stylish shoe was an English-style shoe. Britain's cold, wet weather led to sturdy construction methods in which heavy leather uppers are stitched to thick welted soles, creating substantial, solid-looking shoes that perfectly complemented the period's broad-shouldered, wide-trousered suits. Those high-quality materials and workmanship were necessarily expensive, and they remain so. There's no way around the fact: Cheap shoes always and only look like cheap shoes, which is why the rich are referred to as well heeled.

In tandem with the post-1980s trend toward slimmer suits, men's dress shoes have also been getting leaner, with narrower toes and thinner soles. Thus today's English or American oxford is a somewhat slighter shoe than its 1920s antecedent, though it's still likely to be stouter than its Italian counterpart. The Italians, coping with Mediterranean sun and a lifestyle that wasn't exactly stiff upper lip, began perfecting light, unconstructed, tailored clothing during the twentieth century and demanded similarly weightless and elegant footwear to go with it. When the country developed a ready-to-wear men's shoe industry after the Second World War, it largely dispensed with stitched-welt construction in favor of gluing fine calfskin uppers directly to single-thickness leather outsoles (don't know your apron from your vamp? Turn to page 85). Marked by superb handcraftsmanship, slipper-like Italian shoes and thin-soled dress boots were especially appropriate companions for the newer suits with their trim trousers and pared-down silhouettes.

The Italians refined casual footwear too, including an all-American classic, the penny loafer. The comfortable slip-on originated as a moccasin-style shoe handmade by Norwegian fishermen during their off season. American tourists discovered it in the mid-1930s, and G. H. Bass first manufactured the Weejun in 1936 (drop the "Nor" from *Norwegian* and you get the derivation). Like blue jeans and the trench coat, the loafer became a timeless, genderless wardrobe staple—and a preppy cliché. Italian manufacturers, most famously Gucci, took the simple slip-on, upgraded the leather, thinned down the sole, elongated the toe, and replaced the coin slot (hence, "penny loafers") with a gleaming bridle-bit seen on playboys and jet-setters since the 1970s. Today, with airline travel still requiring that you expose your feet to strangers, loafers are about the most practical all-around shoe you can buy. Just be sure to part with enough cash to acquire a great pair. After all, one of the first laws of fashion is that nothing undermines the effect of a perfectly good suit more unequivocally than a pair of shoddy lace-ups—or slip-ons.

THE ANATOMY OF FOOTWEAR
THE DRESS SHOE*

A FINE SHOE, LIKE A FINE WATCH, COMBINES MECHANICAL PRECISION WITH HUMAN ARTISTRY. AND AS WITH A WATCH, A GOOD PAIR OF OXFORDS IS A LIFETIME COMPANION.

APRON

A large overlay that covers the area where the toe meets the upper part of the foot.

COUNTER

The half-moon-shaped piece of leather that reinforces the heel.

HEEL

The rear, padded area on the bottom of the foot, as well as the piece at the rear of the shoe that supports the heel cup. The heel should not slip off the wearer's foot.

QUARTER

The continuous side and rear panel that forms the side of the shoe, extending from the vamp in front to the heel in the back.

TOE BOX

The front portion of the shoe that covers the toes. It should have support protecting the toes and should be approximately a half inch longer than the length of the longest toe.

TONGUE

A strip of leather running just under the laces of the shoe all the way to the opening, or throat.

VAMP

The front part of the shoe that includes the toe box and the apron.

*AND OTHER SHOE TERMS YOU SHOULD KNOW

BROGUED
Refers to the holes in a wing tip. They once went all the way through to let Scottish bog water out. The term is a nod to the shoe's origins in the Scottish Highlands (*bróg* is Gaelic for footwear).

GOODYEAR WELT
The sole and the upper of the shoe are stitched together (not glued), resulting in the strongest bond in shoemaking. Because of its construction, a Goodyear welt lends itself to resoling many times over.

LINER
The inside covering of the shoe. It should always be leather, since that's what will be touching your foot.

PATINA
The subtle and desirable variation in color normally found in a pair of much-loved and much-polished old shoes.

WING TIP
The distinctive avian, or peaked, shape of the toepiece of a pair of full brogues.

THE FIVE SHOES EVERYONE NEEDS
THE BOTTOM OF YOUR CLOSET SHOULD LOOK SOMETHING LIKE THIS:

BLACK OXFORDS

The sensible bedrock of the grown man's shoe collection. These will get you through just about every family crisis and black-tie event life can throw at you—provided you keep them in good shape.

BROWN SUEDE BOOTS

They can be desert boots in the goes-with-everything sand color, or they can be Chelsea boots in a warm shade of snuff or chocolate. But whatever they are, they'll be the pair you're most likely reaching for when off duty.

CLASSIC SNEAKERS

The sneaker holds a high place in the annals of American footwear. You need a pair in your closet. And we don't mean that grail pair in lurid colors or the ones designed for running up a mountain. We mean the kind of sneakers you refer to by name, like Jack Purcells or Stan Smiths.

LOAFERS

There are many immutable laws of nature, such as: You need a loafer. Year-round, the official dress shoe of the United States is formal enough for the office and casual enough for the weekend.

STYLISH SANDALS

Blame it on climate change or the casualization of everyday dress, or both, but sandals aren't just for bumming around the beach anymore. From gladiators to clogs, slides to mules, sandals have gone from summertime afterthought to everyday essential. (Need more convincing? Turn to page 98.)

The ORIGINALS

JACK LEMMON AND THE LOAFER

The loafer has been a classic since the debut of the moccasin-style Bass Weejun in 1936. A couple of decades later, refined by the Italians in featherweight leather or suede, dress loafers signaled Continental sophistication on everyone from Aristotle Onassis to Congolese premier Patrice Lumumba. In the 1950s, actor Jack Lemmon personified America's leisurely suburban style in a sport shirt, slacks, and a pair of polished black loafers, while **Elvis** frequently opted for a two-tone slip-on instead of blue suede shoes.

DECODING THE DRESS SHOE
FOOTWEAR THAT TOES THE FORMAL LINE

BLACK CAP-TOE OXFORD	BROWN WING TIP BROGUE	BROWN MONK-STRAP	BROWN PLAIN-TOE DRESS LOAFER

The Hallmarks			
A discreet toecap.	Peaked toecap and curving side seams with perforations.	A buckle-and-strap closure that replaces traditional eyelets and laces.	A slip-on with a high vamp and substantial sole.
Variations			
Black calfskin is classic, but dark brown leather is pretty classy too.	A refined European version—black or cordovan calf with a thin sole and a narrow, elongated toe.	Natty suede and the quirkier two-strap model.	Exotic leather or skin, the mark of a true dandy.
Wear it with			
A good suit in fine worsted or flannel.	Any type of suit except black. With heavier fabrics like tweed and corduroy.	A serious worsted suit—and almost any other style of suit or tailored trouser.	A casual suit, or tailored trousers with a blazer or sport jacket.
Wear it to			
The boardroom. Weddings Inaugurations. Funerals, including your own.	The office. A swank lunch. The polo field.	Work and play—it's a true chameleon.	The airport—you'll get through security faster and still look great when you arrive at your meeting.
Wear it at your own risk			
Anywhere except in town.	With a black suit.	On very formal occasions.	With pennies.

THREE WAYS TO TIE YOUR SHOES

MATHEMATICALLY SPEAKING, THERE ARE MILLIONS OF WAYS TO LACE A SHOE WITH SIX PAIRS OF EYELETS. BUT YOU COULD GET BY WITH THESE THREE.

STRAITLACED

Why: The neatest, most classic look.

How: Run the lace through the lowest set of eyelets so that the ends come out the bottom of the upper. Run one end of the lace up the left side (so that it's hidden from view), and pull it through the top-left eyelet, then pull the other end through the remaining eyelets so that the lace forms straight lines across the shoe.

CRISSCROSS

Why: Strong, lasting support.

How: Run the lace through the lowest set of eyelets so that the ends come out the bottom of the upper. Cross the ends over each other, and enter the next set of eyelets from the bottom. Pull through the ends, and enter the next set of eyelets from the top. Repeat these steps with the remaining eyelets.

OVER-UNDER

Why: Comfortable and easy on the foot.

How: Run the lace through the lowest set of eyelets so that the ends come out the top of the upper. Then cross the ends and enter the next set of eyelets from the bottom. Pull through, and continue to cross the ends of the lace while entering each eyelet from the bottom.

THE STYLE DEFINITION: STRAITLACED

straitlaced \strāt·lāst\ **adj** : 1. A colloquialism originating in England in 1554 that describes an individual who exhibits excessively reserved or, some would say, uptight behavior. Syn: prude, stick-in-the-mud, wet blanket. 2. A method of fastening shoes and other garments with laces that bind two separate pieces by spanning them straight across rather than in a crisscross pattern. A common technique used by Europeans to lace their shoes, it results in a tighter, stronger binding. Also employed by British soldiers looking for a more secure way to fasten their boots.

The ORIGINALS

RAEKWON AND SUEDE SHOES

Most people have at least one suede option on their shoe rack, but few have made suede shoes their thing like the Wu-Tang Clan's Raekwon. Along with group mate and friend **Ghostface Killah**, Raekwon elevated the classic Clarks Wallabee, originally popularized by Jamaican "rude boys," into a hip-hop icon through lyrics, album covers, and increasing outlandish custom dye jobs. Sitting somewhere between sneakers and dress shoes, "Wallys" (as they are affectionately known) are available in smooth leather, but it's the suede version that won over the rap game—and, lately, fashion types too—because of their comfort and versatile dress up/down appeal.

FREQUENTLY ASKED QUESTIONS
THE MYSTERIES OF SUEDE SHOES

HOW SHOULD I WEAR THEM?
In 1924 the Prince of Wales scandalized New York Meadowbrook Country Club in Long Island by sporting brown suede shoes with his flannel suit. Some called them brothel creepers. By the 1930s, however, suede shoes were the mark of a real gentleman. Today they signify a sophisticated and individualistic dresser, someone who cares about his feet as much as the rest of his body.

HOW DO I KNOW IF THEY'RE WELL MADE?
As with any investment, you should quiz the salesman. If they can't speak to the quality of the shoe, move on. The best suede is made from the reverse, or flesh, side of calfskin. Kidskin is also used for dressy shoes because of its fine nap. Don't confuse it with nubuck, which looks quite similar but is made from the exterior side of leather that has been buffed (it's of lesser quality). Remember that a suede shoe is tactile footwear, so work the shoe through your hands. Examine it. You'll know it's a well-made pair if the soles and inner linings are leather and the components are stitched together rather than cemented. Cement-bound shoes will inevitably fall apart, leaving you feeling angry and looking tragic.

WHICH STYLE SHOULD I WEAR?
First decide on color. The very nature of the suede shoe is understated, so no pastels, please. Go with chocolate, cognac, or black in the winter and something light brown or tan in the summer. As far as the style of the shoe goes, the most versatile are derby lace-ups and chukka boots because they all work admirably with both navy and gray suits. You can also throw them on with a pair of jeans, khakis, or corduroys just as easily. Call them the utility infielders of foot dressing.

HOW SHOULD I TAKE CARE OF THEM?

Suede is tougher than it looks. To keep your shoes in prime condition, occasionally apply a protective product, like a weather-resisting spray (just make sure it's silicone-free). In addition, a pair of unvarnished shoe trees should be put in them when they're not on your feet. These will absorb perspiration and help them keep their shape. After wearing, simply brush with a soft-bristle brush (not a wire one, which will wear away the nap). This should be a regular wearing procedure, kind of like changing your car's oil. If they get lightly stained—and they most certainly will—you can brush them with a soft gum eraser, and that should do the trick. Then there's the dreaded drenched shoe. You're bound to run out of luck and have to watch your suede-covered feet suffer through a downpour. Don't fret. Stuff them with paper towels and put them in a dry place for twenty-four hours, then lightly brush back the nap to nurse them back to health. Another handy homespun remedy: You can restore suede shoes by lightly steaming them over boiling water. Or you can leave it to a pro to steam-clean them for you.

> WITH A SUIT, ALWAYS WEAR BIG BRITISH SHOES, THE ONES WITH LARGE WELTS. THERE'S NOTHING WORSE THAN DAINTY LITTLE ITALIAN JOBS AT THE END OF THE LEG LINE.
> —*David Bowie*

A GUIDE TO BOOTS

Given that there are boots for all seasons, occasions, and purposes, it's surprising that most people don't wear them much, trudging through the snow or up a mountain excepted. But because many types of boots have slightly maverick origins, they can be a great way to give your style quotient a raffish kick.

THE DRESS BOOT

Whether lace-up or slip-on, with discreet straps or without, a boot that can be worn with all but the most formal suit must be unembellished.

THE CHELSEA BOOT

The ankle-high slip-on with a pointed toe and a zippered or elasticized side opening was a Mod staple in 1960s London. Worn with a slim suit, these boots will still give you a subtle British Invasion vibe. Casual versions may have rounder toes and more overall heft and look good with jeans and cords.

THE DESERT BOOT

Inspired by crepe-soled footwear worn by British servicemen in Egypt during World War II, the suede or soft-leather lace-up was adopted by American rappers in the 1990s as an alternative to the sneaker. Many contemporary takes on the classic desert boot are natty enough to take you from a creative day job to a nightclub.

THE CHUKKA BOOT

This more substantial relative of the desert book started life on the polo field. Its plain good looks are a fine complement to smart tailored sportswear and even casual suits.

The ORIGINALS

THE BEATLES AND THE CHELSEA BOOT

As if the Beatles need another notch in their belt, the Fab Four are credited with popularizing the Chelsea boot—an ankle-high slip-on with elasticized gussets—although they wore a highly customized version that's more accurately called the Beatle boot. The Liverpudlians had London shoemakers Anello & Davide graft elements of the Spanish flamenco boot onto the traditional Chelsea model. Pair the boots with a Pierre Cardin–inspired collarless suit, and you're ready for a British invasion. Further north in Scotland, actor **Sam Heughan** is showing the Chelsea boot's staying power by pairing them with a suit (and tee) that the Fab Four could have only dreamed of.

HOW TO BUILD AN ESSENTIAL SNEAKER COLLECTION

Over the past 25 years, sneaker collecting has transformed from a niche hobby to a worldwide phenomenon. Growing up, most kids had two or three pairs of sneakers. Today, kids and adults alike fill their closets with them. The key to sneaker collecting is focusing on what you truly love, finding a balance between everyday kicks and ones you'll bust out on special occasions, and then passing on everything else. So whether you are fourteen and just starting out or forty and need to trim down the collection, here are the types of sneakers that are truly collection worthy.

Classic Low-Profile Sneaker

These silhouettes go with everything, and they're socially acceptable at basically any occasion. You can't go wrong with the Adidas Stan Smith or the Samba. But if you've got extra cash to spend, Italy's Golden Goose makes the Super-Star, a luxe upgrade that comes prescuffed.

Hype Sneaker

You know the kind: they're teased out on Instagram weeks in advance before "dropping" at stores with lines around the block or online, where you're sure to battle bots and everyone on the internet just for the opportunity to cop. But if you are lucky enough to score one of these sought-after pairs, you'll not only gain the admiration of savvy passersby but also have a potentially lucrative investment to flip on the aftermarket one day— provided you keep them in the box.

Modern Runner

Running shoes have come a long way since the first running boom in the 1970s. Today carbon fiber plates, Gore-Tex uppers, and all manner of cushioning systems have made them more technical and fashionable, not to mention expensive, than ever. Check out category leaders like Nike, Hoka, and Salomon for styles that look as good as they perform (even if you're just running out for coffee).

OG Runner

What we just said about running shoes having come a long way? Here's where they came from—but what they may lack in R&D they more than make up for in vintage looks that will never go out of style. Try the New Balance 993, Asics Gel-Lyte 3, or Nike Tailwinds, which pair well with your entire wardrobe, from your workout shorts to your go-to office chinos.

Retro Basketball High-Top

One of the primary reasons sneaker collecting has become an obsession for grown-ups who should know better is the fact that Nike (and others) released so many iconic styles during their youth. We're talking shoes like the Air Jordan 3 or Reebok Pump for '80s kids, the Air Jordan XI or the Nike Foamposite Royal for '90s kids, Nike LeBrons for '00s kids, and so on.

FIVE THINGS YOU DIDN'T KNOW ABOUT SNEAKERS

1. In 1916, U.S. Rubber Company trademarked a new rubber-soled shoe. The name Peds was already taken, so it chose Keds instead. The first sneaker was born.

2. Adolf "Adi" Dassler (the founder of Adidas) created the modern running shoe in 1925. It gained massive recognition when Olympic gold medalist Jesse Owens wore a pair to the 1936 games.

3. The NBA banned the first pair of Air Jordans from competition in 1985 because their black-and-red combination did not conform to league uniform rules.

4. Global sneaker sales totaled $152.4 billion in 2022. That's up $150 billion—with a "B"—from what Americans purchased in 2007.

5. According to Guinness World Records, as of May 2012, Jordy Geller of Las Vegas, owns the largest collection of sneakers, topping out at over 2,300 pairs.

The ORIGINALS

WILT CHAMBERLAIN AND THE HIGH-TOP SNEAKER

Wilt Chamberlain, aka the Big Dipper, first laced his canvas-and-rubber high-top Chucks for the Kansas Jayhawks in 1955, the beginning of a career that reinvented basketball. In the 1970s, punk rockers like the Ramones became fans of the sneakers, claiming them as part of their own impudently uncouth style. Today it's neither athletic nor punk to wear Converse, but it is a can't-miss move, as Tyler, the Creator and **Timothée Chalamet** know.

The CLASSICS

THE CHUCK TAYLOR ALL STAR

In 1923, in the first iteration of the modern shoe-endorsement deal, basketball evangelist Charles ("Chuck") Taylor signed on to promote Converse, partnering with the shoe company to make the Chuck Taylor All Star. A star high school player in Indiana, Taylor knew his game: He had also been a journeyman jump shooter for eleven professional seasons. Converse added Taylor's signature to the ankle in 1932, and the canvas-and-rubber shoe has essentially remained the same since (though now it's available in nearly every color and zany pattern known to man). The All Star was the official shoe of the Olympics from 1936 to 1968, and Chucks have functioned off the court as the shoe of American youth for most of the past eighty years. Its devotees include American iconoclasts and mischief makers, from Iggy Pop and Rocky Balboa to N.W.A and Nirvana.

The ORIGINALS

BOB DENVER AND THE SANDAL

Sandals have been around almost since man walked upright, and they were a favorite of Jesus, the ultimate counterculture guy of his time. But somewhere along the line, they became relegated to beachwear and hippie style. In the 1968 film *The Sweet Ride*, Bob Denver showed that they could be stylish too, something that **Idris Elba** continues to remind us of today. Like when he was spotted outside *The Late Show* studios in a $36 pair of slide sandals that, on him, instantly became the coolest thing in Manhattan. Which is no easy feat.

HOW A SHOE SHOULD FIT

Squeezing into a suit that doesn't fit? We've all done it. Squeezing into a shoe that's too tight? Murder. Here's what you need to know to keep your feet happy.

AT THE HEEL
This is the one place where your shoe may hurt initially, but fear not. It'll subside. Your heel should rest comfortably against the back liner without slipping.

AT THE INSTEP
The tongue should rest lightly on the top of your foot, without feeling too much pressure.

AT THE TOE
Your longest toe should rest about a half inch from the front edge of the toe box. You should be able to wiggle your toes slightly.

AT THE ARCH
Extra support is fine here, but the shoe should not rise up so much that pressure is put on your arch.

FIND YOUR SHOE SIZE

• Sit with your foot (in a sock) on a piece of paper with your shinbone at a slightly forward angle.

• Trace around your foot with a pencil.

• Draw parallel lines to mark the outermost points (width and length) of your foot.

• Measure the length to $1/16$ inch.

• Do the same with your other foot.

• Choose the larger foot and subtract $1/16$ to $1/8$ inch from the measurement to allow for error.

Inches	Size
$9^{1/2}$	6.5
$9^{5/8}$	7
$9^{13/16}$	7.5
10	8
$10^{1/8}$	8.5
$10^{5/16}$	9
$10^{1/2}$	9.5
$10^{5/8}$	10
$10^{13/16}$	10.5
11	11
$11^{1/8}$	11.5
$11^{5/16}$	12
$11^{1/2}$	12.5
$11^{5/8}$	13
$11^{13/16}$	13.5
12	14

The RULES

NO ONE YOU WORK WITH SHOULD EVER see your toes or nipples. Please dress accordingly.

POLISHING: THE MATERIALS

You'll need the right tools—just a few, but each with a crucial purpose.

SHOE POLISH
Kiwi wax-based polish is as good a brand as any other. (Cream polishes, applied with a brush, may be easier to use, but they won't give you the same shine.) You don't need every color under the sun. Black, of course; a chestnut or darker brown; and something middling or neutral for light-colored shoes.

WELT BRUSH
Looks like a toothbrush (and you can use one in its place). It's designed to get the grit out of the welt, the seam where the shoe's upper joins the sole. You'd be amazed how much dirt gets in there.

POLISHING CLOTH
Select lint-free cotton or linen. Use the same one for putting on the polish that you use for buffing, regardless of the color you're using. And hang on to it: The longer you use the same cloth, the more it becomes suffused with rich oils and dyes.

POLISHING BRUSH
To get the high shine out of the shoe once you've got all that wax into the leather. Horsehair is recommended.

SOLE DRESSING
The edge of the sole takes a scuffing from doorjambs and sidewalks. Restore the pristine look of your shoes with edge dressing, applied with a small craft brush or a cotton swab.

HOW TO POLISH A SHOE

1

Wipe your shoes down with a damp cloth to remove superficial dirt and stains.

2

Wet the welt brush, and scrub out the entire welt strip.

3

If the shoes need it, apply sole-edge dressing—carefully. If you get it on the uppers, it will stain them permanently. Let the edge dressing dry before going any further.

4

Apply polish, using a circular rubbing motion. You don't need to slather it on. You don't need to be gentle. And the more you rub, the better. Let the polish dry. It should take about five minutes.

5

Buff the entire shoe with a polishing brush. For extra gleam, hold the shoe between your knees, and buff the toe vigorously with a lint-free cloth.

EMERGENCY MEASURES AND LONG-TERM CARE

SHOE TREES

Using a wooden shoe tree is the easiest way to increase the life expectancy of a good pair of shoes. The devices maintain the shoes' shape because they resemble the last—a facsimile of your foot on which shoes are built. But more important, the wood absorbs leather-damaging moisture, which can discolor and crack a shoe as it dries—but only if you choose the less decorative unvarnished ones. Varnished trees look posh, but they don't properly draw moisture—i.e., sweat—out of the leather.

Top marks go to unfinished cedar models with a split toe and a fully shaped heel: These ensure the closest possible fit between shoe and tree. Also, there's no need to own a pair of trees for each pair of shoes. The vital time for using them is the hour or two after you have removed the shoes from your feet. After that, the shoes will have returned to their natural architecture and the trees can be removed.

REPAIR WORK

Invest as much care in choosing a cobbler to resole or reheel your shoes as you did in purchasing them. To prevent permanent damage (or, at the least, outrageous repair costs), have all work done before it's absolutely necessary.

SUEDE

Suede shoes are in a category of their own, since you cannot polish away scuff marks. See page 91 for detailed tips.

WET SHOES

Stuff soaking-wet shoes with paper towels, and dry them away from direct heat. Direct heat can dry the leather too fast, causing it to crack—and once that happens, nothing can save your shoes.

SALT STAINS

The traditional remedy for road-salt stains is a little vinegar and water, applied sparingly.

SHOES AS INVESTMENTS

Cheap shoes are a false bargain. They're made of glue, rubber, and low-grade leather, which often bears scars from shrubs, trees, and barbed wire (the normal hazards of bovine life), and which is rejected out of hand by reputable shoemakers. Good shoes begin with great leather, period. Be prepared to pay for it, down to the sole. But if leather isn't your thing, the development of bioleathers, plant-based alternatives to animal hides, has resulted in some surprisingly elevated alternatives.

Whichever type you choose, once you have invested your hard-earned cash in a quality pair, you're going to want to hang on to them. Put a little time and effort into looking after them, and they'll last longer—and be more comfortable—than any three pairs of cheap clodhoppers.

The RULES

ALWAYS BUY YOUR SHOES AFTER 2:00 P.M., when your feet have swollen to their maximum measurement.

ONE CAN NEVER OWN too many pairs of socks.

OUTERWEAR

A trusty outer garment to wear over our regular kits for extra protection from cold or wet weather is essential. More than with any other garment, outerwear is a matter of basic survival. But for those of us not braving the Yukon, outerwear presents a welcome opportunity to stay warm while flexing a little sartorial muscle.

CONTINUED

CASUAL comfort and versatility often trump formality, thanks mainly to technical improvements in textiles. Puffy yet sleek ski parkas, which take advantage of ripstop nylon shells and synthetic-down insulation, have descended from the slopes to become an urban fashion staple, as have less insulated rain shells. But when wearing a well-made suit with English or Italian shoes, donning one of these pieces of technical gear can create some dissonance, especially if you're trying to pair an acid yellow puffer with navy pinstripes. For a safer bet, look to that winter closet stalwart: the overcoat.

As recently as a few hundred years ago, outerwear most commonly took the form of a cape or mantle, but the overcoat became an increasingly popular alternative as far back as the seventeenth century. It had its beginnings in the humble riding coat, a loose and purely functional garment worn by horsemen and soldiers. The heavy wool greatcoat evolved during the next two hundred years, influenced by military garb. When the world map was being chopped up during the Napoleonic era, for example, the coat was trimmed or lined in fur and decorated with braid and frog-fastenings for an exotic Eastern European look. In the U.S. around the time of the Civil War, it gained shoulder capes and overlapping collars like those on the winter greatcoats for Confederate and Union soldiers (who froze in the bitter cold, nevertheless).

The last half of the nineteenth century was a golden age for dress overcoats, several bearing the names of the British aristocrats and places first associated with them. They include the chesterfield, a slightly tapered coat, in either a single-breasted fly-front or double-breasted style, often with a velvet collar; the raglan, a less formal, loose-fitting coat with full-cut sleeves and no shoulder seam; and the ulster, a double-breasted long overcoat with a large convertible collar and a half or full belt.

The armed services have given us several topcoat

perennials. The trench coat, a British army raincoat, emerged from the muddy battlefields of the First World War to become an evergreen classic. The navy popularized a pair of outerwear's most frequent phoenixes: The peacoat or reefer, a heavy double-breasted jacket in dark-blue wool, was favored by nineteenth-century sailors and worn memorably by Jack Nicholson in the 1973 film *The Last Detail*; and the duffle coat, a three-quarter-length hooded sack fastened with leather loops and horn toggles, which was standard issue in the Royal Navy during the First World War. These days that coat comes in everything from tweed and camel hair to shearling and leather, fabrics that turn it into sophisticated casual wear that can be worn over a suit on less formal occasions.

Perhaps the most popular of all casual cold-weather cover-ups is the parka—or anorak, as its Inuit creators called it. Originally made of animal skins, it was a water- and wind-resistant garment used for hunting and kayaking. The hooded jacket initially became fashionable in a gabardine shell version that skiers began wearing during the Depression, but it was Eddie Bauer, the Seattle sporting goods specialist, who invented the lightweight, quilted, down-filled parka, which he began manufacturing in 1936. In the 1950s, the U.S. military developed the nylon snorkel version, which had a hood that zipped snugly around the face.

Outerwear in general has made full use of improved weaving techniques and of the synthetic fibers that have developed since the first one, nylon, was invented just before the Second World War. Even luxury fabrics such as cashmere are sometimes combined with synthetics or treated with proprietary finishing processes—Teflon laminate, for instance—that waterproof them while leaving them breathable, so you don't get clammy. Because today's coats are lighter in weight and svelter than ever before, you can now keep warm without sacrificing style—or space in your overhead bag.

THE ANATOMY OF
THE ESSENTIAL TOPCOAT

GONE ARE THE DAYS OF THE BULKY GREATCOAT. TODAY'S COATS CONVEY STYLISH SELF-POSSESSION IN A TRIM SILHOUETTE. HERE'S WHAT TO LOOK FOR IN YOUR DRESSIEST, MOST IMPORTANT COLD-WEATHER GARMENT.

THE COLLAR

A simple collar with a notched lapel is classy but unstuffy. A contrasting fabric collar—most often velvet, sometimes fur—is a hallmark of the dressier chesterfield coat that's best for formal occasions and evening wear.

THE SHOULDER

Not too wide, and go easy on the padding or you'll sprout superhero shoulders when you put the coat on over a suit. The overall effect should be crisp but natural.

THE FABRIC

Navy, gray, or black cashmere is serious but not solemn. It's also light but warm enough for all but the most brutal weather. For that you'll need an overcoat, which is made of heavier wool or tweed—20- to 22-ounce cloth as opposed to a topcoat's 17 to 18 ounces. Camel hair is a snappier, less conventional—but still businesslike—alternative to classic dark cashmere.

THE BUTTONS

Three buttons are the cleanest, most classic fastening arrangement. Four buttons create a higher—i.e., slightly more formal—gorge. A button-concealing placket is recommended for a sleeker, more minimalist look.

THE FIT

The modern topcoat should skim the body but never pull or pucker, especially when in motion. It should be the same size as your suit and not a size larger (always try it on over a tailored jacket). The sleeves of your jacket or shirt should never protrude beyond those of the coat.

THE LENGTH

Aim for around the knee. A little above if you like a tailored, trim look—but not so short that you look top-heavy. Below the knee is more traditional, especially for heavier coats like the polo (see page 109), but shouldn't extend past mid-calf. Ankle skimming is strictly for the frontier.

THE COAT: A ROSTER

HOW TO CARE FOR YOUR TOPCOAT

Treat it well and it will last you for many seasons.

1. Hang your coat on a strong wood hanger with broad, contoured shoulder pieces. Let it hang freely.

2. Brush frequently to remove dust, lint, and organic particles.

3. Have spills and stains spot cleaned immediately.

4. Steam your coat whenever it's looking limp. Have it done professionally if you don't own a garment steamer.

5. Dry-clean it only once a year, at the very end of the season immediately before you store it.

6. For long-term storage, put the coat in a full-length, breathable-fabric garment bag.

THE CHESTERFIELD

Named after a well-to-do Regency dandy, the sixth earl of Chesterfield, this calf-length, single-breasted coat has always been a plutocratic kind of garment, thanks to a generally dark demeanor (navy, black, or dark gray) and its most distinctive element, a black velvet collar. This detail was reputedly inspired by late-eighteenth-century French noblemen who wore it to express sympathy silently and with style—for victims of the Reign of Terror.

WEAR IT TO: A gala event.

THE TWEED COAT

In Scottish Gaelic, tweed was called an *clò mòr*, or "the big cloth." When it comes to tweeds, you can get away with a bolder pattern in a coat than you ever could in a suit—as long as you don't layer check over check. A true Prince of Wales check, for example, is a modern classic: large-scale, in shades of red-brown and slate-gray. Cheviot tweed, made from the thick yarn of Cheviot sheep, is a sturdier weave suitable for rough-looking winter overcoats. With a tweed coat, keep the rest of your ensemble low-key and let the coat do all the talking.

WEAR IT TO: A book launch party.

OF CLASSIC OPTIONS

THE POLO COAT

From the early twentieth century until well after the Second World War, the polo coat was the all-enveloping outdoor equivalent of the bathrobe, donned by sportsmen to prevent a chill after sweating in the saddle or on the tennis court. Characterized by its roomy double-breasted cut, big, lumpy patch pockets, and a full or half belt, it is habitually made of a thick plush wool or camel hair to give instant warmth after the melee. Its enduring, vaguely gangsterish appeal—especially in the natural camel color—still has its modern devotees in America.

WEAR IT TO: A Harvard-Yale tailgate party.

THE DUFFLE COAT

The good people of Duffel, Belgium, have been weaving thick, double-faced wool for centuries, but it wasn't until the Royal Navy adopted coats made from the fabric in the early twentieth century that the tiny village was put on the proverbial map. Then as now, these warm but relatively light coats had a capacious hood (which could be worn over a rigid cap) and four horn toggles down the front. Huge numbers of duffles were later sold as military surplus after the Second World War, thus paving the way for their present ubiquity.

WEAR IT TO: Sunday brunch.

THE PEACOAT

You'd be hard-pressed to find any fashion brand that doesn't offer some variation on the peacoat, the double-breasted wool coat with broad lapels and wooden buttons. That's only fitting, considering its global reach. Peacoats have been worn since the eighteenth century by European (and, later, American) sailors of all ranks and classes—"pea" derives from the Dutch word *pij*, the preferred type of cloth for early versions—and like the men who wore them, they went around the world and left their influence everywhere they went.

WEAR IT TO: A loft party.

HOW TO WEAR A COAT
YOU NEED BUT THREE COATS. HERE'S HOW TO WEAR 'EM.

Whether you're making snowmen, desperately trying to keep your suit dry on an evening out, or navigating the winds blowing between the office and the parking garage, a good coat is indispensable. Your choices will boil down to the three types below.

THE PARKA

The classic parka comes in many guises these days. It's best with jeans and casual wear, but it can work with a suit. Just make sure that it's longer than your suit jacket and streamlined. If you need to wear it to the office on a regular basis, a color other than bright orange or red will be more versatile. Don't forget: Limit the logos, chunky exterior zippers, and endless Velcro tabs.

THE EVERYDAY

For most days, you need a coat that multitasks, one that can segue from the office to, say, a ballgame. Try one in a blend of cashmere and technical fabric that makes the jacket feel luxurious but keeps wind and water out. A fly front (where the buttons are hidden) suggests higher quality. Don't forget: Light-colored coats show dirt quickly. Be sure yours is cleaned regularly.

THE FORMAL

When dressing up, a simple single-breasted coat in dark wool (cashmere if you can) will always make the grade. Make sure the coat fits over your suit (have a jacket on when you try it) but don't get too big, lest it look borrowed. The waist should be slightly suppressed—you don't want to look like you're wearing a bathrobe. Don't forget: Use a lint brush before you leave the house.

The ORIGINALS

NEIL YOUNG AND THE PEACOAT

Sailors have worn a version of the peacoat for centuries, but in 1969, Canadian rock legend Neil Young paired his with a corduroy button-down and a black turtleneck and invested the salty jacket with folksy earnestness. More recently, actor **Chris Pine**, on the set of *All the Old Knives* in 2022, channeled major Robert Redford vibes with his popped-collar peacoat, continuing Hollywood's obsession with dapper spies.

The ORIGINALS

RUN-D.M.C. AND THE LEATHER JACKET

Between bomber crews, motorcycle gangs, screen stars, and punk rockers, the leather jacket has had no shortage of fans over the decades. But it's hard to argue that anyone wore it better, or innovated the style in more ways, than Run-D.M.C. Known for injecting a harder edge into the rap genre, and for kicking down the door to mainstream acceptance, the "Tougher Than Leather" trio from New York City loved leather jackets in all their forms. Seen here at the American Music Awards in 1997, Rev. Run and D.M.C. rock black leather blazers (with matching pants, no less) while Jam Master Jay sports one the group's signature leather Adidas track jackets. More recently, **Pedro Pascal** stepped out for the evening in a chocolate brown bomber that looked every bit as cool as the default black leather jacket while exuding a more easygoing vibe.

The CLASSICS

THE LEATHER MOTORCYCLE JACKET

The Perfecto motorcycle jacket was already a quarter century old when Marlon Brando immortalized it in the 1954 biker flick *The Wild One*. The original dates from 1928, when a Harley-Davidson distributor asked Schott Brothers, a Staten Island outerwear manufacturer, to create a leather motorcycle jacket. (The brothers had long branded their raincoats under the name Perfecto, after one of the founders' favorite cigar.) The new jacket was rugged enough to protect a speeding rider from the elements, with a zipper and belted waist to keep out the wind. Schott also designed and produced the leather bomber jacket for the Army Air Corps during the Second World War. Though returning veterans turned the bomber into another civilian menswear staple, it has never attained the Perfecto's status, let alone its subversive edge.

A FEW THINGS YOU DIDN'T KNOW ABOUT SHEARLING

Long the requisite territory of mountain men and folks on the outer edges of style, shearling can't be beat for its utility and look. There is nothing warmer in winter months and, when it's combined with modern lines, no more stylish alternative for surviving the cold. And it's so damn comfortable.

1. SHEARLING PREDATES FASHION. It's believed that Neanderthals invented the practice of using animal skins as clothing to protect themselves against cold European climates, including waterproofing leather.

2. IT DOESN'T GROW ON TREES. To make shearling, hides from yearling lambs are tanned with the wool still attached. It's then trimmed to an even length, usually about a half inch.

3. WOOL IS THE OLDEST HIGH-TECH FIBER. It's durable and stays comfortable over a wide range of temperatures. It's also incredibly light. As a bonus, it stays warm when wet and dries off quickly—and doesn't easily pick up body odor.

4. YOU'RE NOT JUMPING OUT OF PLANES WEARING IT, BUT YOU COULD. The original sheepskin bomber jacket was designed in England in 1926 by a former stuntman from America named Leslie Irvin. He went on to supply parachutes to the Allies during the Second World War, and gave his name to the sheepskin flying jackets that his company produced for Allied bomber crews.

THE SUMMER RAINCOAT

AND OTHER LIGHTWEIGHT SOLUTIONS TO FREAK STORMS, CHILLY NIGHTS, HYPERACTIVE AIR-CONDITIONING, AND ASSORTED SEASONAL HAZARDS

THE RAINCOAT

Wear a standard lined trench coat in the middle of August and you'll sweat straight through your shirt. Opt for an unlined coat that shields you from the elements without weighing you down.

THE GOLF JACKET

Stave off the chill of early morning tee times (or other sporting events) with a close-fitting cotton jacket. Look for wider armholes that maximize movement.

THE WINDBREAKER

A grown person has no business in a poncho, but a zip-up nylon windbreaker lets you weather the fiercest storms without compromising your style.

THE WEEKENDER

For protection against subarctic air-conditioning and increasingly chilly nights, an unlined, all-cotton weekend jacket helps ease the transition to early autumn.

THE (STYLE) HISTORY: WATERPROOF FABRICS

For a long time, they were either functionally nonporous (like rubber) or actively water-repellent (like waxed cotton). But since these coatings work well only on tightly woven fabrics, designers could only make stuff that looked more functional than fashionable. Gore-Tex, a high-tech hydrophobic substance invented in the 1970s, allowed your sweat out and kept rain from getting in, but for years it was only used in sport clothing. Not anymore. Coating wool with Gore-Tex adds wet-weather protection yet allows a luxurious wool suit to still look luxurious.

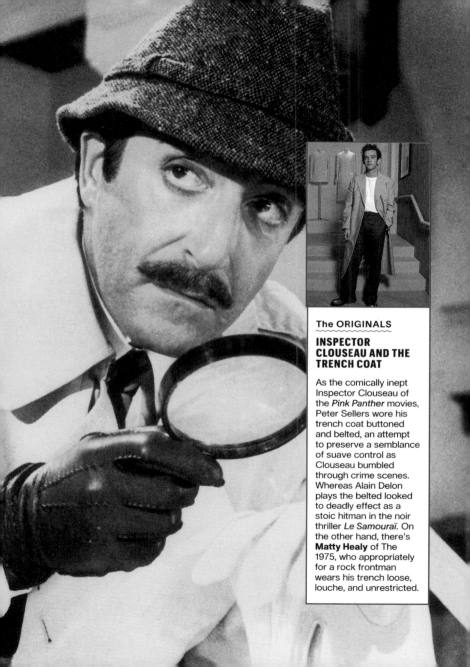

INSPECTOR CLOUSEAU AND THE TRENCH COAT

As the comically inept Inspector Clouseau of the *Pink Panther* movies, Peter Sellers wore his trench coat buttoned and belted, an attempt to preserve a semblance of suave control as Clouseau bumbled through crime scenes. Whereas Alain Delon plays the belted looked to deadly effect as a stoic hitman in the noir thriller *Le Samouraï*. On the other hand, there's **Matty Healy** of The 1975, who appropriately for a rock frontman wears his trench loose, louche, and unrestricted.

WHAT YOU NEED TO KNOW ABOUT
DOWN JACKETS
BUYING A PARKA SUITED FOR THE WHITE-COLLAR WORLD

GOOSE DOWN

Fluffy, natural, and sustainable, it's still the best insulation in terms of warmth-to-weight ratio, compressibility, and longevity. Performance is expressed as fill power, the number of cubic inches an ounce of down occupies, which ranges from 450 (adequate), to 650 (good), to 850 (superlative). The first is more than sufficient for a cold day's stroll in the park; the last will keep you toasty on the summit of K2.

SYNTHETIC DOWN

Goose down loses its insulating properties when it gets wet, and it takes a long time to dry. A good synthetic down like PrimaLoft, which is fluffy like the natural stuff though not as light, will keep you warm even when waterlogged. It's what you need in pouring rain.

FABRICS

The ideal parka shell needs to be water-resistant, windproof, breathable, and down-impermeable. Which means you're best off with synthetic fabrics—nylon, polyester, and laminates such as Gore-Tex. Generally, the more weather-resistant the material, the heavier and costlier it will be. In better jackets, all seams are sealed with protective tape for additional waterproofing.

CONSTRUCTION

In sewn-through or quilted construction, the parka's shell and liner are stitched together to hold the down in place. Although this technique creates cold areas along the lines of stitching, it's adequate for use around town. Baffled construction, in which the down is held in compartments between the shell and the liner, is bulkier and more expensive but much warmer. Don't hit Everest without it.

CLEANING

Dry-cleaning chemicals not only strip the goose down of its natural oils, causing it to break up, but also can damage certain synthetic shell fabrics. Jackets should be laundered in a front-loading washing machine (agitators can rip the shell), using the gentle cycle with warm water and a down-specific detergent. Tumble dry the garment thoroughly at a low heat with two or three tennis balls tossed in to fluff up the down.

STORING

For long-term storage, keep down jackets, loosely folded or on hangers, in breathable cotton or paper bags (never use plastic). Avoid compressing them—it will reduce the down's warmth-giving loft. In the closet, hanging your jacket upside down will prevent the down from bunching along the bottom hem.

The RULES

WEARING A TRASH-BAG PONCHO is actually worse than getting wet.

WEARING WET DOWN IS LIKE WEARING OATMEAL—be sure you have a waterproof shell or a good umbrella.

HOW LAYERS WORK
WARMTH FROM THE INSIDE OUT

(A) Inner Layer ⟶ (B) Middle Layer ⟶ (C) Outer Layer ⟶

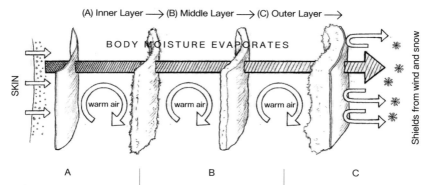

A	B	C
Silk, polypropylene, or another nonabsorbent material draws moisture away from the skin.	Wool, fleece, or another insulating material traps warm air between layers and transfers moisture from one layer to the next.	Gore-Tex, gabardine, or another breathable material lets body moisture escape while staving off wind and water.

DOWN: THE FACTS

Since being invented in the 1930s and 1940s, wind- and water-resistant materials like nylon and polyester have been essential for the outdoors. When stuffed with down, they have become the ultrawarm garments that have helped make extreme mountaineering possible. Here, a few facts:

1. Each cluster of goose down contains dozens of filaments that trap warm air.

2. Its insulating ability is measured in "loft," the number of cubic inches an ounce of down fills.

3. The best down comes from eastern Europe and from the Hutterites, spiritual cousins of the Amish, from the northern Great Plains.

CH

06

ACCESSORIES

A strategically selected coalition of accessories speaks wordlessly to your taste, your stylistic preferences, your position in the world. They are a major component of the extra 10 percent: a statement about yourself that can make an otherwise pedestrian outfit—and you by extension—the object of admiration, respect, even envy.

CONTINUED

ACCESSORIES have another great thing going for them: They pack a big bang for the buck. Take the necktie as an example. After a notable resurgence during the Tumblr-fueled era of dressing up in the early 2010s, known as #menswear, the necktie quickly fell out of favor as streetwear staples like hoodies and tees became de rigueur. The rise of work from home and Zoom calls were the final nails in the necktie's coffin—or so many observers thought. Recently, the humble necktie has once again been popping up on social media and in the look books of influential brands, proving that while the necktie's stock may have fallen for a time, it's more resilient than you may think. And it might even be trendy.

Most of us probably have far more ties than wristwatches—the watch being a potent and often extravagant status symbol. Judging by the mind-boggling range of brands, the celebrity endorsements, and the latent heirloom potential in a watch, selecting and purchasing one can amount to a research project. The earliest watches first appeared in Germany at the end of the fifteenth century; they were spherical, ruinously expensive pieces of jewelry worn on a chain around the neck. Wristwatches were introduced before the First World War but became widely popular only in the 1920s, replacing the pocket watch almost entirely by the end of the Second World War. With the exception of Flavor Flav, most men haven't returned to favoring gaudy chronometers around their necks, but a wristwatch is often the only piece of jewelry many men wear. (Thankfully, this is changing. See your expanded jewelry options on page 168.) You might want to avoid both the wafer-thin and flashy types; plain and elegant should be your watchwords. As for the ubiquitous smartwatch, while seeing your heart rate and email on your wrist has its advantages, they're far outweighed by the fact that you always look like you're about to go for a jog.

As it should be with your cuff links. If you must wear gemstones, do so only with black tie. Even then, they shouldn't be bigger than your thumbnail—the cuff links, that is, not the stones. It's also perfectly stylish to sport unadorned gold or silver ovals or rectangles. In fact, such simplicity is preferable if the cuff links comprise two elements joined by a chain, one for each side of the cuff. But the real point of using cuff links is not display but the fact that they allow you the grown-up privilege of wearing French cuffs.

Some think wearing a formal hat is grown-up too. Emblematic, as opposed to purely protective, male headwear dates to thirteenth-century linen bonnets that tied under the chin. For the next seven hundred years, a gentleman would no more go outdoors hatless than he would shoeless. What he wore on his head was a vital expression of his social position and personal character. Then, in the 1960s, the venerable hat rule was unceremoniously abolished, and men largely gave up their elegant fedoras, crisp homburgs, and soft trilbies as if they were health hazards. These days, you're much more likely to see beanies than bowlers worn—thank God—but some guys can effectively still pull off a brimmed hat that isn't a "dad hat" (aka the baseball hat). If this is you, congrats, just please don't make it your entire personality.

THE ESSENTIAL
ACCESSORIES

WHETHER PURELY PRACTICAL OR OUTRIGHT EMBELLISHMENT, ACCESSORIES ARE WHERE CONFORMITY LEAVES OFF AND INDIVIDUAL EXPRESSION BEGINS. THE RIGHT ONES WILL BRING YOUR WARDROBE INTO SHARP FOCUS.

CASHMERE SCARF
Nothing keeps you warmer or feels better against your skin—or someone else's—than cashmere. Try a bright color or a subdued pattern that contrasts with your overcoat.

KNIT CAP
Commonly known as a beanie, the knit cap can telegraph everything from creative director cool to blue-collar rugged, all while keeping your head warm. Cashmere feels like a small luxury, so go for one in the color of your choice. But don't be the person who wears it in July with a band T-shirt.

LEATHER BELT
Simple elegance is best when choosing a belt. Buckles the size of your wallet and over-the-top hand tooling are best worn to the rodeo. And don't make the biggest mistake: not wearing one at all. You're not fully dressed without one.

LEATHER GLOVES

Choose cashmere-lined supple calf or deerskin for dress, tougher wool-lined cowhide for weekend snowball fights. Throw in a pair of driving gloves if you're so inclined (see page 137).

SILK POCKET SQUARE

Much more than a quaint remnant from your grandfather's day, this diminutive square of fine silk, cotton, or linen—depending on the season and occasion—packs a formidable style punch. Everyone should have at least one. Use it.

SOCKS

It's hard to get excited about socks, but they're an overlooked opportunity to add a splash of color to a monochromatic ensemble. Your best choice for quality: merino wool in winter and Pima cotton in summer.

SUNGLASSES

Once worn only for outdoor sports and in sunny places with beautiful people, sunglasses are now considered an essential weapon in UV protection. It's a bonus that they look so frickin' cool (see pages 133–134).

TIE

The necktie can still be the most expressive piece of cloth in a wardrobe. Consider pattern, width (the wider the tie, the bolder you'll look), fabric (sumptuous silk is still the gold standard), and fold (see pages 124–127).

WALLET

For credit cards only—cash goes in a money clip in your front pocket. A good wallet is not just a place to keep your stuff; it's a source of personal satisfaction.

WATCH

A good timepiece says as much about your status as your shoes. Oh yeah, and it tells time (see pages 128–132).

FREQUENTLY ASKED QUESTIONS
THE TIE
A HISTORY

I'VE ALWAYS HEARD THAT THE NECKTIE STARTED AS SOMETHING TO WIPE YOUR FACE WITH, SORT OF A NAPKIN AROUND THE NECK. TRUE?
No, the origins of knotted neckwear appear to be military: Chinese statues of warriors dating from the third century B.C. show them wearing scarves, apparently as protection from crappy weather. The fabric noose we call a necktie derives more directly from a visit to Paris in about 1660 by a crack military regiment from Croatia. King Louis XIV was so wowed by the brightly colored silk neckerchiefs worn by the Croatian officers that he appropriated the Croat motif as an insignia of royalty and created his own regiment, known as the Royal-Cravates. *Cravate*, of course, is French for "tie." In many countries, using your tie as a napkin is grounds for criminal prosecution and deportation. Here's a tip: Stick it in your shirt when eating.

> A WELL-TIED TIE IS THE FIRST SERIOUS STEP IN LIFE.
> —*Oscar Wilde*

The CLASSICS

THE REPP TIE

You'd be forgiven for assuming the repp is a homegrown American classic like the chino or the penny loafer—its preppie pedigree is as solid as the rocks in a gin and tonic. But the repp originated across the pond, like the trench coat, in the nineteenth century. The British gentry used ties with stripes in strictly prescribed colors and widths to signal the schools, clubs, and regiments they belonged to. During the First World War, the future Duke of Windsor turned the handsome blue-and-red broad-striped tie of his elite Grenadier Guards regiment into a natty fashion accessory that Americans then adopted wholesale. In 1920, Brooks Brothers made a concession to outraged British sensibilities when they ran the diagonal stripes down from right to left, the opposite direction from traditional club and regimental ties. (Today you'll see both configurations.) Stripped of its upstairs-downstairs connotations, the striped repp tie quickly became an American staple, at home in boardrooms and classrooms alike.

KNOTS: A HOW-TO

FOUR-IN-HAND

This is the one you learned for your First Communion, Bar Mitzvah, or other major event in the life of a young boy. Five quick motions and you're done. An easy pinch in the middle gives you a centered dimple. And the skinny knot works well with a button-down.

HALF WINDSOR

Adding a couple of extra moves widens the knot, which works with most collars, and it should be wide enough to fill the center space of your collar.

WINDSOR

Named for the Duke of Windsor, perfected by Frank Sinatra, this is the granddaddy of knots. It takes a little work, yes, but the results will leave others asking how you pulled it off. And with a knot this fat, only a wide spread collar will do.

The RULES

RE: NECKTIES: STOP THE VIOLENCE. You cannot wash them. You cannot iron them. You cannot have them dry-cleaned by just anybody, because they will destroy them. And most important—c'mere so's we can box your ears—you cannot yank them off your neck without untying the knot first, because that will stretch them beyond wearability. Neckties are delicate little creatures, often made of silk that can go for $100 or more a yard, and this is how you treat them?

TIES SHOULD DIMPLE. You want to "train" your ties from the first time you put them on. How: Stick your index finger up into the knot from the front as you tighten, and it should form the coveted cleft.

NO NOVELTY NECKTIES. No novelty anything—novelty having the tendency to wear off.

YOUR TIE KNOT SHOULD ALWAYS conceal the collar band behind it. If it doesn't, it's tied too loose.

THE BOW TIE
EVERY MAN SHOULD KNOW HOW TO DO THIS

1. Make a simple knot with both ends, allowing slightly more length (one or two inches) on the end of A.

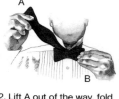

2. Lift A out of the way, fold B into the normal bow shape, and position it on the first knot you made.

3. Drop A vertically over folded end B.

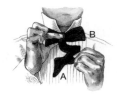

4. Then double A back on itself and position it over the knot so that the two folded ends make a cross.

5. The hard part: Pass folded end A under and behind the left side (yours) of the knot, and through the loop behind folded end B.

6. Tighten the knot you have created, straightening any crumples and creases, particularly in the narrow part at the center.

126

CHARLES EAMES AND THE BOW TIE

The bow tie: for college professors and good ol' boys, right? Charles Eames—with his wife, Ray, the alpha and omega of modern American design—didn't think so. In fact, he never wore anything else around his neck, except a bandanna in the great outdoors. Eames understood that the avant-garde doesn't break from tradition but evolves from it. Speaking of evolving from tradition, **Jonathan Bailey** shows how you can go fully formal today, in this case with a black and brooding mourning suit, and make the bowtie cool again.

The ORIGINALS

STEVE MCQUEEN AND THE WRISTWATCH

There's a term luxury watch collectors, and those who aspire to be, like to use to describe four- and five-figure dive watches: desk divers. That's because despite their impressive water resistance, stainless steel cases, and rugged good looks, most of their owners wouldn't dare use them for anything that could result in a scratch. Steve McQueen, on the other hand, wore all manner of enviable watches while he raced motorcycles and cars and acted in movies that required him to do generally dangerous things. Rocking a T-shirt, stubble, and his Rolex Submariner on the set of *Papillion* in 1973, McQueen makes a compelling case for letting your watches live a little. More recently, chef and model **Rōze Traore** popped up in a Watches of Switzerland ad campaign wearing a tank top, a neckerchief, and a Longines dive watch, as if to prove the point.

FOR EVERY OCCASION, THERE IS THE RIGHT TICKER

HOW TO WEAR A WATCH

There are some timepieces that fit all occasions. But they are rare. Very rare. Much more likely is the scenario in which the watch on your wrist must change with the appointment in your schedule.

FOR HIGH ROLLIN'
Black-tie and other expressly formal events call for a discreet and elegant watch that is small in diameter and slim enough to slip in and out of a French cuff. In this scenario, always match the color of your cuff links to the metal of your watch. If the links are enamel or set with stones, go one better and match the stone of the link to the dial color of the watch's face.

FOR LOUNGIN'
Hang time calls for a big watch to dress up your casual clothes, whether you're in a T-shirt or tweed. Look for a watch in less dressy-looking brushed steel with a chunky body and an interesting face. Bonus points if the watch's pedigree is derived from aviation, sailing, or car racing.

FOR WORKIN'
A chunky chronograph in steel or yellow gold makes a bold statement across a conference table. Only you can decide how flashy you should go, but remember to match the links.

FOR SWEATIN'
You may have a gutsy, top-of-the-line steel chronograph from a great Swiss maker. It may have a host of macho functions, but be sensible and leave it at home. The smart choice is a feature-packed sports watch, like a GPS model that can tell you exactly how far you've run, or a smartwatch that captures all manner of fitness data for you to pour over later. Of course you can always go old school and get a digital watch with a simple stopwatch function and some water resistance that won't break the bank, or your heart if you drop a kettlebell on it.

The RULES

YOU MAY NEVER LEARN to use a tachymeter, but it looks cool, regardless.

ALWAYS OPT FOR A SAPPHIRE CRYSTAL. It's virtually scratch-proof, so you can actually tell the time.

THERE IS A DIFFERENCE BETWEEN water-resistant and waterproof. This is usually learned the hard way.

SLEEK WATCHES ON LEATHER STRAPS LOOK BEST FOR dressing up, and heavier metal-link bracelets go better with casual clothing.

CLOSE-UP ON LUXURY WATCHES
SEVEN IMPORTANT QUESTIONS TO ASK YOURSELF BEFORE YOU GO OUT AND DROP BIG COIN

TOURBILLION
Invented two hundred years ago, the elite mechanism corrects for gravity.

ROTOR
In a self-winding mechanical watch, it spins in response to the wearer's wrist movements.

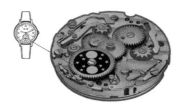

MOON PHASE
An example of a complicated function in a mechanical watch.

1. SPLURGE OR NOT?
Luxury mechanical watches range from under $1,000 to $100,000 and more. Among the most expensive are the prized tourbillions, which only an elite group of master watchmakers has the skills to produce. (The two-hundred-year-old mechanism consists of a revolving carriage that holds the balance wheel and escapement and makes a complete turn every sixty seconds to average out timekeeping errors caused by gravity.) Ultimately, a watch is a status symbol.

2. ROSE, WHITE, OR YELLOW GOLD?
The tint of a piece of gold depends on the proportion of copper and silver mixed with the pure gold. Yellow will always be stylish, but you might consider one of the myriad rose-gold options. Rose has the most copper of the three golds, which gives it a soft, pinkish hue.

3. STEEL OR TITANIUM?
High-grade stainless steel is strong, shiny, and highly resistant to rust and corrosion. But titanium is 30 percent stronger and 50 percent lighter than steel, more corrosion resistant, antimagnetic, and even hypoallergenic. A titanium watch does feel amazingly light and comfortable on the wrist, but the trade-off is a subdued—some say dull—gray watch that, for all its strength, scratches easily.

4. SIMPLE OR COMPLICATED?
In watchmaking terms, a complication is any function beyond simple time telling in a mechanical watch, such as a calendar or a moon-phase indicator. Usually, though, the term refers to sophisticated mechanisms like perpetual calendars and split-second chronographs, which contain hundreds of tiny hand-assembled parts. Because they're so labor-intensive, complicated watches are expensive and prized for the feats they perform.

5. HOW BIG?

Men's wristwatches have grown as if on steroids; they broke the 40-millimeter-diameter barrier at the turn of this century. The reason? Mostly style. The trend was largely inspired by the reissue of an old Italian diver's watch, which was originally designed large so it could be read underwater. That said, small is gaining steam. Inspired by vintage styles, makers and collectors alike are gravitating toward diameters as low as 36 millimeters. It all depends on preference—and your wrist size.

6. DO I NEED A CHRONOGRAPH?

Most guys prize chronographs—timepieces with a stopwatch function—thanks to the macho, sporty look of all those buttons and subdials. They are also functional and can time an event to one fifth of a second for mechanical chronos and to one hundredth of a second in digital quartz chronos. But unless you've just signed up for the Ironman, they're mostly for adornment.

7. WATER RESISTANCE: FIVE BARS OR TWENTY?

Watches have different levels of water resistance, indicated on the dial or case back. Pay close attention to the fine print because the depth units are anything but universal. Most companies give water resistance in meters. Occasionally you'll come across ATMs (for atmospheres) or bars, both of which are equal to ten meters. Once you've done the math, choose a depth based on your needs. Water-resistant to fifty meters means you can wear it in the shower. Sports watches generally have one hundred-meter (swimming, snorkeling) or two hundred-meter (recreational scuba diving) water resistance. You don't need more than that unless you intend to wear the watch while deep-sea diving.

A GUIDE TO WATCH CARE

Get your mechanical watch serviced at a good repair shop every few years. Professionals will strip down the movement, clean it with ultrasound equipment, oil the works, tighten or change the waterproof joints, and polish the case. Find an authorized shop through your brand's website.

Avoid exposing your watch to extreme heat or cold. That means removing it before entering saunas or snowball fights.

Watches with leather straps shouldn't be worn every day. They need to be aired out between wears so that the leather can dry.

Change the battery on your quartz watch every three years. Ignore this benchmark and your battery could start leaking acid, corroding the interior of your watch. Then it will no longer work.

Even if your watch is self-winding, wind it once every few weeks to keep the wheels in motion and the oils fluid.

There is nothing wrong with a watch that can be cured by shaking the hell out of it.

KNOW THE DIFFERENCE

MECHANICAL VS. QUARTZ

MECHANICAL
A timepiece whose movement is powered by a mainspring connected to a system of gears, wheels, and weights. The hands of mechanical watches move smoothly around the face. However, because of the high number of moving parts, they gain or lose a few seconds per day and about one hour per year in accuracy. Mechanical watches involve a high degree of craftsmanship and inhabit the upper echelons of watchmaking.

QUARTZ
Unlike a mechanical watch, a quartz watch has fewer moving parts and is regulated by an electrified sliver of quartz, which vibrates at a constant rate when charged. It is inexpensive to make and exceedingly accurate, losing on average only one minute of accuracy per year.

A quartz movement can be identified immediately by following the movement of the watch's hands, which jump from second to second instead of sweeping fluidly like those of mechanical watches.

The CLASSICS

THE OMEGA SPEEDMASTER

For a Swiss watch, the Speedmaster is a peculiarly American success story. The Omega Speedmaster Professional Chronograph debuted in 1957 and was selected by NASA technicians in 1965 as the only watch qualified for all crewed space missions. It graced the wrists of every Apollo crew member from then on. It was the first watch worn on the moon during the Apollo 11 mission—thus earning its nickname, Moon Watch (the original stainless steel band was replaced with Velcro to enable it to fit over the sleeve of a space suit). Its moment of true glory came in 1970, when its consistent timekeeping saved the lives of the crew of Apollo 13, including Jim Lovell, who used its chronograph functions to time the firing of the secondary rockets that guided the disabled spacecraft through reentry. With its movie-star looks—classic stainless steel case, black face, and three interior dials—the Speedmaster has won cameo roles in films ranging from The Right Stuff to Stowaway, with Daniel Dae Kim.

The CLASSICS

THE RAY-BAN WAYFARER

By 1983, when Tom Cruise wore his in *Risky Business*, the Ray-Ban Wayfarer already meant West Coast cool. Derived from a smaller, leaner 1950s original, Cruise's screen frames embodied the swaggering, top-down prosperity of the decade. Ray-Ban's original wire-framed Aviator, adopted by the air force during the Second World War and famously worn by General Douglas MacArthur, still gets long-term plaudits from style gurus. But the Wayfarer, more deeply suffused with Hollywood meaning, deserves the cooler props. It was designed in 1952 by inventor Raymond Stegeman, whose patent drawing reveals the original Wayfarer in a decidedly goofier, cat-glasses shape typical of 1950s design. By 1961, when Audrey Hepburn wore a pair in *Breakfast at Tiffany's,* the frames had grown into their trademark silhouette, generously proportioned yet streamlined. Since then, film and rock stars, including Bob Dylan, Jack Nicholson, Robert Pattinson, Pharrell Williams, and Bruno Mars, have embraced the Wayfarer as a signature accessory—or a perfect disguise.

YOU'VE GOT NOWHERE TO PUT YOUR SUNGLASSES

OPTION 1

Don't rotate them upward so they're sitting on top of your head. Instead, make sure the protective case that came with your sunglasses is always in your briefcase or workbag. Get in the habit of using it.

OPTION 2

No briefcase? If you're wearing a suit or a jacket, put your sunglasses in your top inside pocket, with the lenses facing out for optimal protection. Stowing in any other pocket increases the risk of frame damage or lens scratching.

OPTION 3

No jacket? Lay the glasses on the table, lenses up. Admire them occasionally. Do not forget them when you get up to leave.

The RULES

TAKE YOUR SHADES OFF when speaking to someone who's not wearing any. It's a trust issue.

The ORIGINALS

TOM CRUISE AND THE SIGNATURE SUNGLASSES

In 1983's Risky Business, Tom Cruise was a teenage dork before he discovered the power of a pair of Ray-Ban Wayfarers. That year, 360,000 pairs of the famous shades were sold, up from only 18,000 in 1981—a fact that speaks to the magic of product placement and a star in Ray-Bans. As the Blues Brothers, **John Belushi and Dan Aykroyd** began wearing Wayfarers in 1978, channeling the look of blues legends like John Lee Hooker and Ray Charles.

YOUR EYEGLASSES

SHOULD CONTRAST, NOT IMITATE, THE SHAPE OF YOUR FACE. HERE'S A QUICK GUIDE:

YOUR SHAPE: HEART

YOUR SPECS: A heart-shaped face already has a lot of definition. Since your head is top-heavy, go for a geometric frame that gives some width to the lower half of your face.

YOUR SHAPE: SQUARE

YOUR SPECS: Since a square face already has angles, go for a round or oval frame that shapes your cheekbones. A decorative frame with width will often do the trick.

YOUR SHAPE: ROUND

YOUR SPECS: Avoid dark frames; they only make your face appear heavy. A round face needs direction, so opt for angular and narrow frames—never a square or a circle.

YOUR SHAPE: OVAL

YOUR SPECS: A modern rectangle is best for an oval face. Because your face is longer than it is wide, you'll need frames that provide width. If your face is wider than it is long, go the opposite way.

The ORIGINALS

ANDRÉ 3000 AND THE EXTRA 10 PERCENT

André is the modern style icon par excellence, with an eye for telling sartorial details that pull everything together—like a diamond-pane silk scarf that mediates between a tweed herringbone jacket and a monochrome turtleneck. Even if you never dress remotely like him, you could do worse than follow his example of reining in flamboyant color and old-school preppy by pairing them with classic tailoring. **Billy Porter's** red carpet tuxedo gown certainly doesn't qualify as classic tailoring, but then again, sometimes you don't need an extra 10 percent, you need an extra 10,000.

THE HAND THAT ROCKS

FOUR STEPS TO INSULATING YOUR FINGERS

Your hand's size is measured from its circumference at the knuckles. Find out what it is, and buy accordingly.

The inside is as important as the outside. Look for a knitted cashmere lining.

Gloves don't have to match your clothes but should at least complement your wardrobe. Black and brown are the most versatile choices.

Leather needs care if it's going to last. If gloves get wet, don't dry them on a heater, which would desiccate the leather.

A CELEBRATION OF UTTER UTILITY
BOILED-WOOL MITTENS

You probably traded your mittens for gloves when you turned ten and never looked back. Good for you. But as any polar explorer with ten fingers can tell you, boiled-wool mittens are among the simplest and most effective ways of shielding your hands from the cold. The best kinds are made from pure knit wool that's been boiled to create a dense, feltlike fabric that insulates better than most other untreated woods or leathers. They're tough, naturally water-resistant, and all but windproof, and because wool "breathes" and releases moisture, heat-sapping sweat won't build up on your hands. No cutting-edge fabrics. No twenty-first-century bells and whistles. Just wool and hot water. But for those long waits on the train platform or the overtime nail-biter at Lambeau, there's nothing warmer.

THE WAY OF THE SCARF

THE NOVICE
A rakish wrap that warms the neck and the sternum.

THE LOOPHOLE
The modern sophisticate's choice. Here, asymmetry is key.

THE WHIPLASH CLASSIC
Also looks great tucked into a suit.

THE LOOPHOLE
The modern sophisticate's choice. Here, asymmetry is key.

THE NEW CASUAL

CH

07

In a world where anything goes, this is how to navigate our very laid-back zeitgeist and build a wardrobe that works anywhere.

CONTINUED

THE ERA of casual Fridays and clear demarcations between work and weekend wear are in our recent past, but culturally they might as well be part of the Pleistocene. Whether it's because of the rise of athleisure, the wholesale takeover of the luxury industry by streetwear, or that little global event that endeared us all to loungewear in ways we couldn't have predicted, it's impossible not to notice the permissiveness of casual dressing these days. Ties have been dumped faster than crypto, sneakers are spotted in the Oval Office, and the suit's obituary has been written again and again (for the record: reports of its death have been greatly exaggerated). While this sartorial sea change might cause some traditionalist hand-wringing, for those of us not still debating the ideal Oxford collar roll—yes, that's a thing people do—the expansion of the modern man's wardrobe offers a level of freedom and creativity unheard of just a decade ago. And we are, as they say, here for it.

Yet even as the rules continue to relax or disappear, it's good to keep some guardrails in mind to help you maneuver through menswear's new normal.

KNOW THYSELF. Epictetus nailed it (in A.D. 108., no less) when he suggested, "Know, first, who you are; and then adorn yourself accordingly." You can be Gorpcore on the weekends and Stealth Wealth at the office (more on those in a bit), but by establishing a personal style center you always come back to, you'll not only build a lasting wardrobe of casual essentials but also create a frame of reference for when you want to experiment. Like you, your style should mature and evolve over the years, but also like you, there should be a fixed point in your style firmament to act as a North Star, to keep you from wandering too far afield.

INVEST IN QUALITY. Yes, you've heard this one before (in the pages of this book, for example), but it was probably in relation to a finely tailored suit or an investment-worthy watch. These days, quality comes in many forms—consider the fact that the phrase *luxury sneakers* is no longer an oxymoron—which means that you should apply this axiom to your casual wear with the same intent as you would traditional investment pieces. That means skipping the fast-fashion purveyors and mall brands (as your wallet allows) in favor of something with a little more substance. All your hoodies don't need to be cashmere, but investing in quality casual pieces will upgrade your closet and likely prevent you from turning it over every season or two, which benefits the planet as much as your personal style.

DON'T FORGET TO HAVE FUN. We live in an increasingly serious world, where just checking the news can be viewed as an act of courage. And while we don't see the art of dressing yourself every day as a frivolity, we've also been happy to move beyond menswear's punctilious past. If you bought heavy into minimalism, try a maximalist piece to shake things up. Stuck in the somber end of the color spectrum? See what a bubblegum pink or canary yellow can do for you. And if you've been debating whether you can pull off a piece of jewelry, just go for it. We all deserve more fun these days.

THE CASUAL CONTINUUM

FROM JUSTIN BIEBER TO MICHAEL B. JORDAN, THERE'S A WIDER SPECTRUM THAN EVER FOR WHAT CONSTITUTES DRESSING CASUALLY. SEE WHERE YOU FALL.

WILDLY CASUAL

Hot-pink sweatsuit, Oakley wrap sunglasses, a satin Lakers jacket. When Justin Bieber steps out, it's anyone's guess what he's going to show up in, but it's definitely, unrepentantly going to be wildly casual. As the saying goes: "Trained professional, do not attempt."

WILDLY CASUAL

ADVENTUROUS CASUAL

Donald Glover is one of the most stylish men of our era because he's adroit at mixing staple pieces, like a black tee and retro Nike sneakers, with curveball moves like a Donald Duck cardigan from Gucci. It's adventurous without going overboard.

EVERYDAY CASUAL

Ryan Reynolds is the sweet spot of casual dressing. With his tailored chinos, subdued tees, and flex-y, but not too flex-y, suede jackets, he's ready for pretty much any scenario, every day.

SHARP CASUAL

It's not dressed up, it's taking Everyday Casual and putting an edge on it. By pairing a nontraditional suit color with an easy-going striped shirt and white leather sneakers, Tom Holland looks as relaxed as he does professional.

FORMAL CASUAL

FORMAL CASUAL

What's the opposite of Bieber's IDGAF style? Michael B. Jordan's casual approach to formal dressing. The leading man turns it out on the red carpet by choosing tailored clothing in boundary-pushing colors, patterns, and fabrics.

IF YOU'VE GOT A T-SHIRT WITH BLOODSTAINS ALL OVER IT, MAYBE LAUNDRY ISN'T YOUR BIGGEST PROBLEM.
—*Jerry Seinfeld*

THE (REVISED) CLASSICS

FROM ESSENTIALS YOU CAN ALWAYS LEAN ON TO A FEW NEW KEY PIECES TO LEVEL UP WITH, LET THESE BE THE FOUNDATIONAL PIECES YOU BUILD YOUR CASUAL LOOKS UPON.

SHORTS

Not the kind you might mow the lawn in, we're talking shorts worthy of an NBA tunnel walk, like when LeBron James rocks a pair of dress shorts by designer Thom Browne. But we're not advocating for price point here as much as we are diversity. Mix in with your chino pairs some inspired by outdoor gear, ones that show off a little extra leg, a pair in a suiting fabric.

A LIGHT JACKET

Baracuta to bomber, chore to coach's, trucker to trench. Whatever you choose—and you certainly don't have to choose just one—the light jacket instantly pulls together your outfit while also performing its functional duty.

TEES

This American icon continues to be undefeated. The T-shirt's staying power lies in its simplicity and versatility, and these days you can choose from refined tees that can easily sub in for a dress shirt under a blazer or a suit, or vintage throwbacks and designer graphics that are meant to showcase your personal style.

THE BAG

For a while there, bags got a bad rap (remember the "European carryall"?), but then guys realized that pockets can do only so much of the heavy lifting. Whether it's a streamlined backpack to keep your hands free to scroll or any one of the modern takes on the waist bag (née, fanny pack) your stuff deserves to be carried in style.

SNEAKERS

Not the mint condition collectibles or the ultra-techy gym pair, we're talking about something with a minimalist vibe: clean, classic, and maybe a little muted. Think Chucks or Vans, or something with Italian leather. These sneakers don't scream hype but whisper quiet confidence. (Want to know how to build a sneaker collection? Turn to page 94.)

ATHLETIC-INSPIRED STYLES

Sport's influence on fashion (and vice versa) has never been greater, so from tees designed with brunching and benching in mind to luxe new takes on varsity classics, athletic-inspired gear adds a fashionable, functional element to your outfits.

CHINOS AND JEANS

Just because your grandfather (and your great-grandfather) wore them doesn't mean you need to wear these wardrobe workhorses the same way. Chinos and jeans come in a panoply of fits, fabrics, and colors.

LAYERING PIECES

The most stylish men you can think of all have one go-to move in common: layering. That's because layered looks are just more visually interesting, plus they easily adapt to multiple environments, both social and meteorological. So stock up on pieces that can do double or triple duty, like cardigans, Henleys, vests, etc.

SIGNATURE JEWELRY

Jewelry is just another platform for showcasing your style, which means you can dial it up or down as you like. Find your signature piece—think Michael Jordan's single hoop earring—and you'll have an individual statement that also acts as the ultimate accessory.

FIT FINDER

FIGURE OUT THE FIT—FROM SLIM TO SLOUCHY— THAT WORKS BEST FOR YOU.

Athletic

Great For: Gym rats or any guy who needs a little extra room to move around in.

Watch Out For: Off-balance proportions—that is, clothing that accommodates wider biceps and thighs but stays slim everywhere else (you'll end up looking like MMA fighter Conor McGregor in one of his famous suits).

Oversize

Great For: Making a big—no pun intended—style statement.

Watch Out For: Cartoonishly large fits that make you stand out—and not in a good way.

Slim

Great For: Leaner body types and anyone looking for a clean, polished silhouette.

Watch Out For: Skinny fits from the 2010s, which are dated but also restricting.

Classic

Great For: Easing into more relaxed fits or for guys with larger builds.

Watch Out For: Boxy, shapeless cuts, unless you're embracing Norm-core (see page 155 for more).

Relaxed

Great For: Getting in on menswear trends and staying very, very comfortable.

Watch Out For: Taking it too far. By not tempering relaxed pieces with more tailored ones, you run the risk of looking sloppy.

BEYOND SLIM

IF YOU'VE BEEN WEARING A SLIM CUT FOR ONLY THE LAST DECADE OR SO IT'S HIGH TIME TO TRY SOME LOOSER FITS. HERE'S THE RIGHT WAY TO GET IN ON MENSWEAR'S NEW DIRECTION.

TURN UP THE VOLUME

➤ Embrace proportion play to take a walk on the wide side with pieces that complement, not completely replace, your existing wardrobe. Start with a wide-leg pair of dress pants or a classic straight-fit pair of jeans, like Levi's iconic 501 fit. They might feel a little strange at first, but here's where the "play" part comes in: pair with them a regular-fitting (not tight)sweater, tee, or button-up in your closet. You'll get the effect of wearing a more voluminous cut without feeling overwhelmed by suddenly going relaxed all over. The approach works in the reverse too when you pair a slouchy sweatshirt, a denim jacket, or even a sport coat with a pair of regular-fit (not skinny) pants. If you're finding that a wider-leg pant is making you look short or sloppy, try a high-waist pair with a bit of a crop, or try tucking your top in. Either way, the result will be a cleaner line and a visually elongating result.

DO AS GRANDPA DID

➤ Pleats and elasticized waistbands are suddenly everywhere, from mall brands to European runways, which means they're not just for pensioners and post-Thanksgiving naps anymore. The difference between today's versions and those of yesteryear comes down to intentionality, with designers strategically adding them to augment an already stylish pair of pants. Pleats create volume, so the number of them is in direct proportion to how much you want up top. Single are the safest bet to maintain a trim appearance, whereas double introduces some noticeable room (and triple are only for those willing to really commit). Look for a subtle taper from the knee down to keep the vibe polished. As for elastic waistbands, it's as easy as looking for a traditional pair of dress pants, in a refined suiting fabric like a solid-color worsted wool or a patterned tweed, and then opting for the elasticized version, which can be worn as a separate or even with a jacket. One thing to note, though: Since these waists look gathered and often feature a sweats-like drawstring, keeping your top untucked is advisable, lest anyone discover your comfy secret.

THE SPECTRUM OF
SWEATPANTS

HAS ANY PIECE OF MENSWEAR EVER SEEN ITS STOCK RISE SO METEORICALLY? NOW THAT WE'RE LIVING IN THE GOLDEN ERA OF SWEATS, IT'S TIME TO DISSECT THE DIFFERENCES BETWEEN THE FIVE PAIRS YOUR CLOSET NEEDS.

CLASSIC

Think: Champion. The kind of sweats that used to come in only heather gray and served as the OG athletic uniform.

ATHLEISURE

When sweats decided to come off the couch, this is what they became. The same level of comfort with a serious upgrade in looks, like slimmer fits and modern details.

TECHNICAL

Borrowing from both outdoor gear and performance sportswear, these are the tricked-out pairs suitable for actually getting physical in, with their moisture-wicking fabrics and articulated cuts.

STREETWEAR

Classic sweats have always been part of the streetwear canon. But now that the category has grown up, today's versions retain the swagger but add a design sensibility with artist collaborations and collectible graphics.

LUXURY

What you'd wear to fly . . . private. With some featuring fabrics you might associate more with high-end knits, like cashmere, these certainly banish sweatpants' schlubby reputation.

STRETCH: A REDEMPTION STORY

HOW A TEXTILE INNOVATION WENT FROM REVILED TO RESPECTED (SORT OF)

It infiltrated Oxfords, snuck into sweaters, and climbed into chinos. Most distressingly, to purists at least, it has come to dominate the denim market. We're talking about stretch, an additive fiber that, depending on where you stand, is either a lifestyle godsend or an affront to good taste. The controversy around stretch is a more recent story, but the history of stretch fabrics isn't. The chemical giant DuPont introduced synthetic stockings for women, replacing the traditional silk, way back in 1938. (It's worth pausing to acknowledge that apprehension, or even downright opposition, to wearing stretch fabrics seems to be a purely male hangup.) Following the overwhelming success of their "nylons," DuPont struck gold again with the development of spandex, the stretchy, shiny fiber that became synonymous with aerobics culture in the '80s and the fodder for every cyclist joke ever. Wrapping a small percentage of elastane (the nonbranded name for spandex or Lycra) around more traditional fibers, like cotton, provides the finished fabric with a degree of stretch and retention—the ability of a fabric to bounce back to its original shape—not found in 100 percent natural-fiber content fabrics. In 1987, the *New York Times* called stretch fabrics "the most important new development in fashion," and in the ensuing decades they've helped athletes perform and everyone from cancer survivors to non-gender-conforming people feel more comfortable in their bodies. So what's the beef? George Hahn, the actor whose sharp style we've featured in "How We Dress Now," once wryly called stretch "The High-Fructose Corn Syrup of Menswear" in a post on his site, reflecting a growing chorus of opposition. As menswear got slimmer in the '00s and '10s, stretch fabrics made it possible for guys of all sizes to comfortably wear trimmer cuts— arguably a good thing. But some of the very people preaching the tailored look,

like the extremely online traditionalists of the #menswear movement, also venerated authenticity in all things (see: selvedge denim), meaning stretch was sneered at. Meanwhile, even those not deeply invested in style forums tended to be adverse toward any clothing with a perceived whiff of the feminine. Stretch jeans, aka the target of the hottest takes, were deemed too shiny, too plasticky, and just too weird for serious consideration. Fast-forward a few years, and the pandemic suddenly recalibrated everyone's appetite for comfort just as marketers perfected their stretch euphemisms, borrowing the language of sports to make the fabrics more palatable to male consumers. Today stretch is a ubiquitous part of the menswear market, likely in your closet in ways you don't suspect and hopefully don't care about. Because if a tiny fiber can make you look better and feel better about yourself, those are the only stretch facts that matter.

FREQUENTLY ASKED QUESTIONS: CARGO PANTS

I HEARD IT'S COOL TO WEAR CARGO PANTS AGAIN. CAN THAT BE TRUE?

Short answer: Yes! After several years of banishment into the menswear wilderness, the humble cargo pants are back, which is good news for guys who never understood why they became verboten in the first place. (Truth is, they never went away; they just became overshadowed by the saggy, garishly logoed worst of the bunch.) Today's cargos aren't that, they're also not the slim-fit versions of the #menswear era. Instead, they're somewhere in the middle, with even the baggier ones cut to drape perfectly. If it's been awhile, ease back in with a military-influenced BDU (battle dress uniform) pair in a classic shade of olive. They'll typically have a straight, or even slightly tapered, leg that works well with everything from polos to chunky knits. Or embrace the weirder end of the renaissance with plenty of tech-wear influences, like integrated web belts, water-repellent fabrics, and pockets of all shapes, sizes, and placements, along with an indulgently loose fit. Whichever you choose, wear them with pride—and don't let anyone take your cargos away again.

MODERN OFFICE STYLE

HOW TO LOOK PUT TOGETHER, EVEN IF YOUR COLLEAGUES AREN'T

DRIVE AT THE SPEED OF TRAFFIC

You know that saying about the safest speed to drive being the one that everyone else is going (we're not sure this applies on the autobahn)? That's true of your office as well. When in doubt, take stock

FREQUENTLY ASKED QUESTIONS: SANDALS

I WANT A PAIR OF STYLISH SANDALS BUT HAVE ONLY EVER WORN FLIP-FLOPS. HELP!
Far be it for us to neg on the flip-flop, a style that has been around since 4,000 B.C. and is the undisputed king of amusement parks, resort pools, and beachside bars everywhere. But there's something almost too casual about them—maybe it's all that exposed foot—to be considered truly stylish. Enter: the slide. You may remember them from college bathrooms and beach cabanas,

of what everyone else is doing, especially those in the C-suite, and calibrate yourself accordingly. Buttoned-up law firm? Stick to dark-toned suits and a pair of wing tips. Digital marketing agency? Opt for a chore coat and a pair of chunky-soled loafers instead. Zigging while everyone zags might get you noticed, but going with the sartorial flow will keep the attention on your contributions, not your style flexes.

WHEN IN DOUBT, OVERDRESS

If you've surveyed the landscape and you're still not sure which gear to be in, shift into fifth. But take note, what we're advocating for here isn't the buttoned-up look in a traditional sense. Rather, it's a strategic deployment of its elements to raise your profile above the rest of the cubicle dwellers. Like a trim knitted polo, which you can

throw a perfectly tailored navy suit over. Pull on a pair of dress boots, and you're suddenly known as the well-dressed one in the office.

GO HIGH/LOW

One of the best style moves you can master, in or out of the office, is what's known in the biz as high/low. The idea is simple: Take one piece that's basic, and pair it with something that's decidedly not. For example, wear your Italian double-breasted blazer with a pair of high tops, or a vintage military jacket with some tailored wool trousers. Most of all, don't overthink it.

IT'S CASUAL, NOT SLOPPY

Yes, you can get away with a lot these days at work—depending on where you work—but that doesn't mean you should show up in the

same clothes as your WFH days. The jeans can stay, and so can the graphic tee, but they should be creative enough to make an impact while remaining professional enough that they doesn't set off the wrong alarm bells. Just put a little polish on the whole look with proper lace-up shoes and a toned-down shirt jacket and you're golden.

FIND YOUR FOOTWEAR

We've given you a lot to think about, so we're going to do you a favor and not add to the pile with this one. When it comes to your footwear, find your style and stick with it. Whether they're bench-made leather dress shoes or the latest hype sneaker drop, if it works for you, then be consistent with the application and you'll at least get credit for being the person who always wears great ____.

but in the last few years professional athletes started to flaunt luxury styles on game day while models shod in avant-garde iterations trekked down runways. That's good news for us regular folk, who have plenty of options to choose from, including chunky, cushy models with a futuristic vibe to full-grain leather ones with a sleek silhouette. Of course, you can never go wrong with a pair from Germany's Birkenstock, who've successfully moved beyond the Vermont

pottery teacher associations to offer some of the coolest sandal styles out there, from the lightweight EVA Arizona model to the classic suede Boston (which is technically a clog, but who's keeping score?). It's worth mentioning, though, that where you can go wrong is wearing sandals to the office. Unless you live in Hawaii, it's best to keep your feet covered during quarterly earnings calls.

WE DEFINE SOME OF MENSWEAR'S MOST TALKED ABOUT
RECENT TRENDS—AND LET YOU KNOW IF THEY'RE WORTH
INVESTING IN.

THE NEW
CASUAL GLOSSARY

Dad-core

Baseball hats, relaxed-fit chinos, those dove gray
New Balances for running or mowing the lawn (or
both)—that's Dad-core. As fatherhood itself has
gone through a rebrand, so has its uniform, and what
was once considered schlubby has now been embraced as stylish. That's a good thing, because dad
style was always about simple, hard-wearing pieces
that fit the life you were living, not some aspirational
fantasy. Now you'll find some of the coolest names
in menswear stocking Dad-core favorites like light-
wash denim and cardigan sweaters, but you can just
as easily head to your favorite vintage shop and pick

them up. Dad would probably applaud the move for its sound financial judgment.

The verdict: Take a cue from actual dads and embrace Dad-core with earnestness, not irony.

Gorp-core

A funny thing happened a few years back. Fleece jackets jumped from New England campuses and food co-ops everywhere to New York Fashion Week. Then in 2020, Drake and designer Virgil Abloh showed up to one of those shows in matching technical parkas, and suddenly everyone was all in on Gorp-core (an acronym for "good old raisins and peanuts," aka trail mix). Citrusy-colored rain shells were now considered streetwear, collaboration puffer jackets proliferated, and the aforementioned fleece could be found as easily in luxury European boutiques and niche Japanese menswear stores as in REI. Gorp-core's appeal lies in its cozy, unfussy functionality—because even if you're not summiting Denali, who doesn't want to feel like they could?

THE VERDICT: Mixing outdoor apparel with more traditional or even tailored pieces isn't just a stylish move; it's a practical one too.

Norm-core

OK, bear with us here for a moment: Dad-core is Norm-core, but Norm-core is not Dad-core (and Gorp-core is kinda both). Norm-core appeared on the scene in 2014 as an ironic anti-trend that was as much fueled by Instagram and the media's at-

→ CONTINUED

CONTINUED

tempt to explain it as it was actual people wearing actual clothes. Norm-core is most often described as Jerry Seinfeld's look from his eponymous '90s sitcom. But it's really a catch-all for a style redolent of people who don't follow, or even know about, fashion trends. In conclusion, Norm-core is anything that fashionable people don't consider fashionable, thereby making it paradoxically fashionable. Got that?

The verdict: You can channel Norm-core's retro vibes without succumbing to dressing like a meme.

Scumbro

Esquire dubbed 2018 the Summer of Sleaze, and for good reason. Famous, wildly successful men like Justin Bieber and Pete Davidson suddenly started dressing like teenage weed dealers. Paparazzi captured them in nylon shorts, track pants, oversize hoodies, and washed-out logo tees while sporting greasy hair, all the shades of hair dye, and wispy mustaches the likes most of us haven't seen

since junior high. Over the years, the Scumbro aesthetic has matured, in a manner of speaking, into a 1970s-flavored look we call "Lotharibro," which favors gold accessories, high-waisted trousers, drapey shirts with baroque prints, and some strategic skin baring (the mustache remains, but in a fuller, fluffier incarnation).

The verdict: Go ahead, add a little louche to your look. But take it easy on the sleazy.

Stealth Wealth

Think *Succession*. An impeccable array of what could be described as ultra-luxury basics, like logo-less baseball hats, monochromatic tees, and minimalist outerwear, with a blandness that belies their price tags (which can soar into the five figures). Stealth Wealth is considered the ultimate flex because only you know that your black crewneck sweater is the equivalent of a month's rent for a four-bedroom Manhattan condo.

The verdict: We endorse the understated style, if not the eye-watering retail.

THE ANATOMY OF
FLEECE

MENSWEAR'S LOVE AFFAIR WITH THE COZY, VERSATILE STAPLE OF TRAILHEADS EVERYWHERE HAS TAKEN THE HUMBLE FLEECE TO WHOLE NEW HEIGHTS OF FUNCTIONALITY AND STYLISHNESS.

THE FABRIC

If you're of a certain age, you may remember when almost every fleece seemed to be a Polartec fleece. That's because in 1981 the company changed the outerwear game by inventing a fabric knit from synthetic fibers, first used by the outfitting legends at Patagonia in their (still stylish) Snap-T fleece jackets. Lofty and hydrophobic, polyester fleece is great for keeping warm and staying comfortable, but its petroleum-based origins make it dubious for the environment. That's why many brands now choose to use recycled PET (polyethylene terephthalate), sourced from discarded plastic bottles.

THE FIT

Fleece jackets were originally designed for layering, so many have a roomy fit that can accommodate a sweatshirt or flannel underneath. However, trimmer versions are available that can be worn like a sweater with just a T-shirt or Henley. Of course, you can also go the opposite direction with many brands offering oversized fleeces, to really get your teddy bear on.

THE STYLE

Fleece styles break down into two camps: zip-ups and pullovers. Which you choose is really a personal preference, but zip-ups do tend to lend themselves more naturally to being worn as a jacket, with their on/off ease, whereas pullover styles are best for layering or used as true outdoor gear. We should also mention the fleece vest, which has its place . . . mostly on the backs of Wall Street bros. If you didn't get one for free, co-branded with your firm's logo, they're best avoided.

THE DETAILS

Like all clothing meant to endure backwoods extremes, fleece jackets were designed with functional elements, many of which can still be found on even the most fashionable iterations today. We're talking underarm gussets (for ease of movement), pit zips (to avoid overheating), bungee cord cinches (to customize the fit), and, depending on the model, zip-in compatibility (to pair with a shell for warmth). Some fleeces also sport DWR (durable water repellent) finishes to protect you from light precipitation, and things like stand collars and elasticized cuffs (to block chilly gusts).

159

THE NEW CASUAL RULES

FORGET (MOST OF) WHAT YOU'VE HEARD. FROM A WORK TRIP TO A WEDDING, HERE'S WHAT YOU NEED TO KNOW TO PULL OFF A STYLISHLY CASUAL LOOK IN ANY SCENARIO.

ON A FLIGHT

Once upon a time, people dressed up to soar through the heavens. Decades later, a smaller group of people chided the rest of us for not continuing that hoary tradition. Sure, dressing like Don Draper to fly Delta sounds appealing until you remember that you're on the red-eye in coach, not a DC-10 eating steak au poivre off bone china. Realistically, when flying, you should aim for a blend of comfort, functionality, and a few polished touches to avoid the popular sleepaway camp look of rocking a sweatsuit while clutching your bed pillow. You'll find that most brands, from high to low, make a version of the "travel" blazer: an unstructured jacket cut in wool or cotton mixed with a stretch fiber, like elastane, for ease of movement. Some versions feature antimicrobial treatments (to fight odors), wrinkle-resistant fabrics (to survive the overhead bin), and extra pockets (to keep your passport handy). If you're on a work trip, you can head straight to the client presentation and no one will be the wiser. If you're not, consider it a sharper take on the essential light jacket. Pair it with an elastic or tie waist pair of dress pants in a relaxed cut of wool, which is both breathable and naturally moisture resistant, or a pair of soft cotton chinos. Make sure to pack a solid-color cashmere sweater in your carry-on, since it will not only keep you warm in-flight, but

you can also wear it in lieu of the blazer when you land.

Loafers or a minimalist pair of slip-on sneakers will save you time and frustration while going through security (just please keep them on during the ride). You don't have to go luxury (although it doesn't hurt), but investing in a high-quality suitcase will ensure that you'll have it for years and maybe even draw a few envious stares in the terminal.

A DAY AT THE BEACH

From giant logoed swim trunks that graze the calves to sunglasses best left to Guy Fieri, never has so little clothing gone so wrong. But it doesn't have to be that way. Instead, think of a day of sun and sand as an opportunity to flaunt your personal style in the same way you would on the streets, just less of it.

Start by assessing what state your beach bod is in and how much leg you're comfortable baring. You don't need to look like a stunt double from an *Avengers* spinoff, but a relaxed cut will be more forgiving than a trim trunk. When it comes to length, most guys overcompensate. Whatever you think you're comfortable with, consider going one length shorter. It gives off a more athletic appearance, but it's also more comfortable than those basketball shorts–size mon-

CONTINUED

strosities that flap in the sea breeze.

Now that you have your fit right, consider color. We're living in a golden age of swimwear, which means that your options range from tasteful geometrics to high-volume florals to every shade of the rainbow. Even if you skew reserved in your everyday style, an eye-catching pair of swim trunks is an easy way to get out of your comfort zone with minimal risk. When choosing footwear, skip the old sneakers or chewed-up flip-flops and opt for a pair of designer slides or classic canvas espadrilles. A light sweatshirt will keep you warm when the sun goes down, and the on-trend terry cloth polo is comfortable and exudes retro cabana vibes. Finally, a word on those sunglasses: There are far too many styles to discuss here, but let's just say that no man has ever been wronged by a pair of Wayfarers (see page 133 for more on the timeless style).

DATE NIGHT

Whether it's with your life partner or your latest app swipe, date night often either paralyzes guys with fear or sends them scurrying to one end of the style spectrum. Instead, you should take your inspiration from rapper A$AP Rocky, who always manages to nail the right balance between dressy and comfortable. And that's really the zone you want to play in because while date night represents the opportunity to do a little sartorial stunting, you're not going to fully enjoy yourself—and we want you to enjoy yourself—if you're feeling constricted or self-conscious. The old rule was to always wear a collared shirt, maybe even a tie and jacket, and definitely a pair of polished hard bottoms. That's certainly not a wrong answer, but let's consider Rocky's look that was captured on the streets of L.A. shortly after he became a dad. Yes, the tie is still there, but it's an ornate print you might have seen in the '80s, and the blazer has been swapped for a muted navy jacket that feels more functional. He's got on a crisp white shirt, but it's tucked into a pair of relaxed "dad" jeans (see our discussion of Dad-core, page 154) and he adds a personal touch with the dollar sign belt buckle—and a joint dangling from his mouth. Check local laws before proceeding with that last one, but the point is that he looks great while also looking self-assured and at ease, two things that dates are known to find very attractive.

→ CONTINUED

WEDDINGS

Before we go any further, let's just put it out there that if you're the one getting married, we encourage you to rage against the wedding-industrial complex and have whatever damn kind of ceremony you want (*Lord of the Rings* themed? Do you). But you really should consider wearing a suit, preferably custom made, and in a style you'll keep for decades. OK, now that we've gotten that out of the way, let's keep this focused on the myriad dress codes you'll likely encounter during a typical wedding season as a guest (see page 28). Couples used to keep it to "black tie" or "semiformal," so things were easy, but we now live in the age of "psychedelic garden party," so it's a little more complicated but also a lot more fun. "Black tie" is the most traditional, and it means you'll need to wear a tux. Donald Glover can get away with brown velvet, but mere mortals should usually stick to black wool. "Black-tie optional" means that, yes, you can wear a normal suit, but keep it in the black/navy/gray range. Sorry, but "semiformal" still means suit, although now you've been given the liberty to play with fabric and color, depending on the season (warmer = lighter; colder = darker). "Cocktail" is where things start to loosen up, which means you don't even need a full suit or tie. You should, however, still stick to a collared shirt and nothing too loud (and no sneakers just yet). "Beach formal" or "dressy casual"? Now it's time to play—within reason. Ditch the tie or the collared shirt entirely, and lighten up the suit color, but keep your footwear respectable and your accessories tasteful. "Casual" or "psychedelic garden party"? Go nuts and wear sneakers, but remember that you're still attending the union of two people for life, so no shorts—and definitely no Crocs.

THE HOLIDAYS

Holiday style is a fine line: Go too casual and you'll draw Grandma's stink eye, but tip too dressy and you risk getting roasted by your cousins. Conventional style wisdom used to be that a Fair Isle sweater or velvet blazer could get you through Thanksgiving dinners and holiday work parties alike, but are you really investing in a jacket you can roll out only once a year? Instead, approach any holiday event as you would a wedding. That is, consider who's throwing it and what their expectations are—and then add a festive spin of your own. If your boss rented out a Michelin-starred restaurant for a fete in the city, lose the office suit and instead opt for a subtly patterned wool (like houndstooth) or corduroy (the thinner the wale, or ridges, the dressier it is) blazer in a slightly relaxed fit with pair of dark wool pants, no jeans. Instead of a shirt-and-tie combo, go for a turtleneck sweater in merino or cashmere, and don't be afraid to experiment with a holiday-appropriate plaid scarf, pocket square, or other accessory (just one, though). Black combat-style boots or thick-soled brogues, like Doc Martens, pair nicely and also keep your feet dry on the snowy walk to the train. On the other hand, if dinner is a potluck at Aunt Linda's condo, your goal is to add some spark while not blowing everyone out of the water. Don't bother with the blazer. Here, you want something that's respectful yet laid-back, like a fuzzy mohair cardigan with a slouchy fit, or the classic fisherman cable-knit sweater in a modern, seasonal color. Jeans are kosher in this situation, but stick to dark or lightly washed colors, which are more dressed up, and no baggy fits. Clean low-key sneakers or suede boots complete the look, as does a vintage-inspired dive watch or slim silver bracelet, and you'll stay in Grandma's good graces.

The ORIGINALS

JAMES DEAN AND THE WHITE T-SHIRT

Leave it to Dean, who fueled his short career on the allure of wayward youth, to make the plain white T-shirt the uniform of cool, brooding guys everywhere. When another rebel, Marlon Brando, wore one in the 1951 movie *A Streetcar Named Desire,* he made fashion and retail history: The humble undergarment became an instant sportswear classic, and more than 180 million were sold by the end of the year. These days the white tee is resurgent yet again, thanks to actor **Jeremy Allen White's** character on *The Bear,* which sent the internet into a frenzy to determine the provenance of his particularly well-fitting tee.

JEWELRY 101

IN CASE YOU HAVEN'T NOTICED, MORE MEN ARE WEARING JEWELRY—AND WE DON'T MEAN WATCHES AND WEDDING RINGS. A POWERFUL WAY TO MAKE A PERSONAL STYLE STATEMENT, JEWELRY MIGHT JUST BE MENSWEAR'S NEWEST, AND COOLEST, "THIRD PIECE."

CHAINS AND NECKLACES

Low risk with a high reward, there's a reason why everyone from TikTok influencers to break-out actors are rocking chains. Necklaces used to have a raffish '70s feel to them, or an '80s rapper vibe, but—guess what—both of those are worth emulating now. For the former, look for thinner links in gold or silver, while the latter definitely calls for chunking it up, maybe with a pendant or some precious stones. Either way, adding this accessory will draw attention to your neckline (which means you need to pay more attention to your facial hair and skin-care routines too), so think about what you're wearing it with and what you want the look to say. Speaking of rappers, you may have been surprised to see some of your favorites recently sporting pearls. No longer just a staple of your grandma's jewelry box, pearl necklaces from designers like Vivienne Westwood are a next-level style flex for guys who no longer care about upholding fusty gender norms.

A WORD ON TATTOOS

Biker, punk, deviant, criminal. These are a few of the connotations that tattoos used to carry for those who dared get one. But now your boss has one, and so does your waiter, your partner, your nanny, and your neighbors (and possibly you too). Does that mean tattoos are stylish? That depends as much on the person who got inked as the ink itself. Take David Beckham. The former footballer is a modern style icon and a walking art gallery, with more than 60 tattoos to date, including lions, cherubs, crucifixes, Chinese, Hebrew, and Sanskrit. Are they the coolest tattoos we've ever seen? No, but paired with his consistently impeccable style, not to mention his various genetic gifts, they've become as essential to his look as the perfectly tailored suits. Then there's rapper Post Malone, whose 78-plus tattoos wouldn't look out of place in a notorious Russian prison. They're definitely out there (see: his "zombie Jesus" chest piece), but so is his maximalist style, so for him it works. Tattoos might be the ultimate individualist accessory because they often hold a significance specific to you. But unlike jewelry or clothing, they never come off. So whether you're thinking of getting your first or wondering if there's any space left for the next, know that it's as much about how you pull them off as what they are.

RINGS

This is probably where your mind first goes when you hear *jewelry,* thanks to that aforementioned wedding ring. But hitched or not, rings are a simple yet powerful way to add personality to any look. And we do mean any look, because the right ring, or rings, will quickly become something you'll feel naked without. A good rule of, uh, thumb is to consider your hand and finger size, as larger hands typically require larger pieces. Rings are also infused with symbolism (there's that wedding ring again), so consider what a signet vs. a skull says about you. Nothing says you can't mix your metals, but if you're wearing multiple rings, consider sticking to one material for a harmonious look. Finally, whatever you do, do it with confidence, especially if you're going skull.

EARRINGS

The underrated accessory of the modern man, earrings are where expression and aesthetics intersect—plus, there's just something hardcore about having a permanent hole in your ear. From Will Smith to Harry Styles, earrings have become the go-to accessory for guys looking to flaunt their personal style. Whether you go hoops or studs, dangly or dainty, there are a few things to keep in mind when choosing the right pair for you. First, you're going to be wearing them all day, so consider the weight. You want to feel comfortable with them in, not as if your head is being pulled down by two kettlebells. Second, studs and small hoops fly under the radar as classic, while dangly earrings and large hoops command statement-making attention. That said, this move is all about style, so don't be afraid of a little flash.

BRACELETS

Go back a decade in menswear and you'll find plenty of peacocking bloggers up to their elbows in rope bracelets. Thankfully, that era has passed, but what hasn't gone of our style is a well-chosen bracelet. In fact, because their profile resembles a wristwatch, bracelets have long been strategically deployed by stylish guys who want a little something extra (also, like wristwatches, they can discreetly disappear underneath cuffs). Like everything else we've discussed, bracelets can go large scale or small, be "attention- grabbing" or elegantly whisper. They're also easy to wear, either as a substitute for a watch or a complement to one. Like other accessories, they're meant to work in tandem with what you've already got on. Heading to the office? An 18-karat gold cuff looks great peeking out from a crisp, white shirt. Headed to the beach? A candy-colored beaded bracelet matches the mood of a terry cloth polo and some board shorts. You also don't have to wear only one, but mind that stack.

PERSONAL CARE

CH 08

Long gone are the days when you could just shave, comb your hair, and call it a day. So is the retrograde view that taking care of yourself is somehow "unmanly." Modern living does a number on you, so consider a personal care routine to be as much about maintenance and prevention as it is about looking your best.

→
CONTINUED

How we groom ourselves will always reflect our times, and let's face it, times are feeling a little different right now. Thanks to cell phones and social media, we're seeing a lot more of our face, our hair, and every other part of us. Along with that comes endless ways to dissect and critique what's being posted. At the same time, once woo-woo concepts like self-care and wellness have entered our everyday lexicon, as is the welcome idea that hairy or smooth, light skinned or dark, we should celebrate our unique features rather than try to hide or change them. You know those bottles of shampoo-conditioner-bodywash, the kind that you'll find in the grooming aisle of your chain pharmacy or big-box store? They owe their existence to a one-size-fits all philosophy that feels antiquated and ineffective. Besides, they all smell like a dorm shower.

To build a great personal care regime, start at the top. If you already have a barber you love, great. If not, don't be afraid to try a few shops until you find The One—and when you do, take care of that man or woman like they're your best friend. (Because when it comes to looking good, they kind of are.) Pay them a regular visit to keep your chosen style looking fresh, especially before big events like interviews or weddings. Closer to home, make an honest assessment of your hair needs and select your products accordingly. Short and curly requires a different approach than long and straight; ask you barber if you're unsure. And if you're losing it, know that while your options have expanded, the best thing you can do is to own it (same goes with graying hair).

Thanks to the sheer volume of product options, skin care can be daunting at best and confusing at worst. Maybe that's why many guys have no skin-care routine to speak of—they don't want to put in the effort to figure it out. Or maybe they just don't care. Well, they should, and so should you. Good skin care is one of the most powerful tools we have against most of the common issues men face on their faces: acne, wrinkles, even sun damage (your daily moisturizer has SPF, right?). Effective skin care takes more than washing your face with whatever soap you have lying around and hoping for the best. It's like anything worthwhile: It takes commitment, consistency, and care, not to mention a healthy amount of experimentation till you find the right products for you. Thankfully, building a skin-care routine from ground zero takes only a few simple steps, and you'd be surprised by how much of a difference you'll see after a few weeks of following them.

As for minding the rest of you, from how to take care of your nails to finding your signature scent, men's grooming is now an entire category unto itself (in fact, we release our annual Grooming Awards to help guide you through it). So book a spa appointment, try a few new creams, and don't be afraid of a little pampering. Yes, the idea is to look good, but the secret that all these things feel great too.

THE BATHROOM
ESSENTIALS
WHAT DOES YOUR BATHROOM HAVE IN IT? EXAMINE OUR LIST, AND CHECK WHERE APPLICABLE.

AFTERSHAVE BALM
Restores moisture to the skin and relieves mild post-shave irritation. Avoid products with a high alcohol content.

ALCOHOL-FREE DEODORANT
Smelling clean is just as important as looking good—but not at the expense of cracked armpits. Avoid the drying effects of alcohol.

BADGER-HAIR SHAVING BRUSH
Gives your face the optimum slippery protection from the razor blade.

BODY WASH
It won't slip out of your hands in the shower, it smells good, and unlike soap, it travels well.

CONDITIONER
No, it's not a waste of time—it makes your hair softer and less dry in winter. It may even help control dandruff.

HAIRSTYLING PRODUCT
It comes in many forms—more on those in a bit—but whichever you choose, make sure you have some on hand to keep your preferred hairstyle, and flyaways in place.

HAND-AND-BODY LOTION
Odysseus used olive oil. You should use something that doesn't make you smell like salad.

NAIL CLIPPERS
Keep those fingers and toes from looking feral.

RAZOR
Three blades? Five? Forget the gizmos. Find a handsome razor that's well-balanced and is compatible with good blades.

SHAMPOO
Find one that's suitable for your hair type, and use it every second or third day (unless you're training for the Iron Man—then it's every day).

SHAVING CREAM
Creams and gels that come in aerosol cans dry your skin. Find one in a tub or jar that preferably contains lanolin or a hypoallergenic substitute.

SOAP
All soap washes off dirt and bacteria—you don't need deodorant and antibacterial soaps. Those made from a base of vegetable glycerin are kinder to your face.

SPF 15 LIP BALM
Lips burn too. Just like ears. Use an SPF balm to protect from the sun's rays and prevent cracking in winter.

SPF 15 MOISTURIZER
The sun is stronger—and you're exposed to it more often—than you think. Use it every day, and consider bumping up to SPF 30 or above for even more protection.

YOUR HAIR HAS A LIFE OF ITS OWN

HOW TO DEAL WITH THE INEVITABLE: GRAYING, OVERLY STYLED, AND THINNING HAIR

MY GRAYING HAIR MAKES ME LOOK FIFTEEN YEARS OLDER THAN I AM. WHAT SHOULD I DO?

As we said, the best reaction to graying hair is to own it ("silver fox" is a compliment, after all). But if you can't accept it, the next-best thing to do is dye it. Thanks to improved technology, which makes for drastically shorter dyeing time and greater subtlety, a huge number of men are turning to color jobs. You probably even know a couple of guys who do it, and you have no idea because modern dyes camouflage the gray rather than completely cover it, and fade out gradually over time. Getting it done once every two haircuts should be plenty—it's a ten-minute rinse at the washbasin. We strongly recommend going to a salon, but if you must do it at home, remember: Most people think their hair is darker than it really is. So when choosing your color, grab one shade lighter. Expect to leave the dye in for a little less than the recommended time if you have fine hair. And although we don't suggest going against the instructions, no matter how long you leave it in, it's difficult to overdye your hair. Unless, of course, you're Rudy Giuliani.

WHEN I USE GEL, MY HAIR LOOKS TOO "STYLED."

First, where did you buy your gel? If it came in a jumbo container from Costco, you may be damaging more than just your image. Cheap gel strips hair and causes dryness. Trash it. You probably shouldn't be

using gel at all. If you want a natural look—but nothing too shabby—opt for creams. They're softer on your hair than gels. For more hold, use pastes or waxes. Apply a little—a good dime-size drop—then add more as you need to. Your hair should be damp before it takes on a shape. Emulsify product in your palm and apply to the roots, working your way out. Then use your hands to style, and never a brush or a blow-dryer.

I'M LOSING MY HAIR. AND IT MAKES ME SAD.

The only dignified way to deal with balding or thinning hair is to learn to live with it. Nay, learn to love it. Confidence (and a good cut) is more attractive than any treatment. Trying to conceal it will only draw attention, generally of the pointing, laughing, and snickering variety. Never create length to hide thinning hair; the longer it is, the skimpier it looks. You want a short-cropped cut, which will make your hair appear thicker. Or you can forget all of the above and do what Bruce Willis did: Use a disposable razor. Shave every other day, or even every day if you want that nice, intimidating shine. Just don't forget the sunscreen.

If you're too proud, stubborn, or deluded to admit defeat, you have two options: Good (expensive) transplants have come so far that even hair professionals often can't tell the difference. There's also finasteride, minoxidil, stem cells, and even lasers to apply to your dome in the hopes of coaxing those follicles back into action. Which one is right for you? Ask your doctor, who can also steer you away from the snake oil.

> ### The RULES
> NO GROUP OF PEOPLE HAVE WORSE HAIRSTYLES THAN POLITICIANS.

The ORIGINALS

HAIR ENVY: JOHN F. KENNEDY JR.

He had it all: the dynastic family name, the buzzy magazine, and the New York social pages lifestyle with wife Carolyn Bessette. He also had incredible hair. The tousled mane JFK Jr. sported during his youth in Hyannis Port gave way to a more kept, yet no less luxurious, hairstyle as an adult in Manhattan, a look that reflected his boyish charm. We still miss it . . . but when we need a dose we look to **Dev Patel**, whose follicular gifts abound.

FIVE TERMS TO USE WITH YOUR BARBER

YOU KNOW HOW YOU WANT YOUR HAIR TO LOOK, BUT YOU DON'T KNOW HOW TO EXPLAIN IT. HERE ARE FIVE TERMS YOUR BARBER WILL UNDERSTAND.

THINNED OUT
When the barber breaks out thinning shears (which look like regular scissors but have matching sets of "teeth" with gaps between them), which allow some of the hairs to be cut short and others to remain at their full length. Good for thick, unmanageable hair.

TAPERED (OR TAPE-UP)
Not to be confused with the fade, a taper (or "tape-up," as it's commonly called) refers to a cut that is longer on top but gradually tapers down the sides of the head to the hairline, where it's the shortest.

LAYERED
When longer hair rests on top of shorter hair, and your hair appears to have some movement and depth. Good for thin hair.

FADED
Perhaps the most popular barbershop move, fades work for all types of hair. You just need to know which kind of fade you're after: low (starts at your hairline), medium (starts around your ears), or high (between the top of the ears and your temples). Note that fades are only for the sides of your head, so you still need to know what you're doing up top.

FLAT TOP AND HIGH TOP
Originally called the crew cut, the flat top is a military-influenced style that features close-cut sides and a short, yes, flat appearance up top. The high top is the same cut but with more verticality (Celtics star Jaylen Brown has been known to wear one).

RAZORED
When a barber uses a razor (instead of scissors) to trim the ends of your hair. Your hairs will have a tapered edge (rather than a blunt, straight-cut edge), which will give them more texture and volume.

**THE HAIRCUT RULES,
OR HOW NOT TO LOOK LIKE A JERK AT THE SALON**

· Great haircuts result from great cutters of hair and from a consistent working relationship with a barber or stylist who knows your taste and needs. Such people are unlikely to provide their services for ten bucks. · Never come straight from the gym. A good gauge of the appeal of your hair is the amount of time the assistant runs water on your head before touching you. The longer it runs, the more you should consider regular bathing. · If you're offered a robe, be sure to take off your collared shirt. It makes your stylist's job easier. · It's fine to read a magazine or a book, but your cell phone should stay in your pocket. · Although it is perfectly acceptable to request a particular stylist, it's creepy when you ask for a favorite shampoo assistant. · Tip your stylist at least 20 percent. More around the holidays will get you special consideration the rest of the year for things like free touch-ups and preferential scheduling. For your hair washer, never tip less than five dollars.

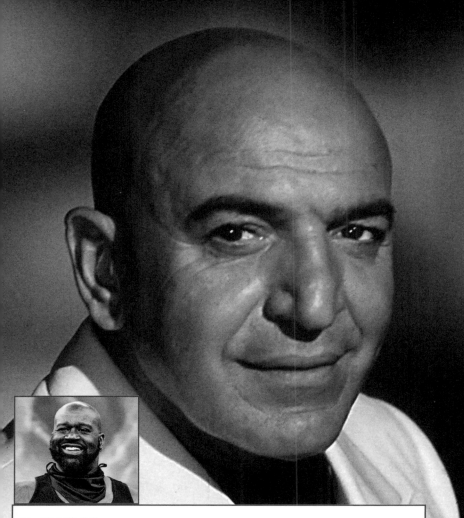

BALD AND BEAUTIFUL: TELLY SAVALAS

In the 1970s, Aristotelis "Telly" Savalas accomplished an amazing feat: He made going bald seem not only cool but badass. Playing the role of NYPD Lt. Theodopolus "Theo" Kojak, Savalas turned an entire generation on to the radical notion that an actor didn't need hair to be a star or to be seen as a sex symbol. Savalas opened the door to baldness as a signature look, and in the decades that followed, many famous men ran through it, including Michael Jordan, Bruce Willis, Common, **Shaquille O'Neal**, Dwayne "The Rock" Johnson, and Stanley Tucci.

THE SUGGESTION

MIND THE BEARD LINE

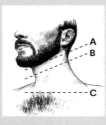

Many years ago, growing a beard was easy. You just stopped shaving. Where your beard ended—chin, neck, or somewhere after your chest hair began—was nobody's concern, least of all yours. Now beards are a noted accessory, and thus require more tailoring. Stopped too close to the jawbone (line A), a beard makes you look uptight. Left to wander down your neck (line C), however, a beard invites comparisons to feral creatures or communist firebrands. The safest bet is the one-inch band just above your Adam's apple (line B). Here you manage to have both a legitimate beard and something of a neck.

HOW TO
SHAVE

THE AVERAGE GUY WILL SHAVE ABOUT 20,000 TIMES IN HIS LIFETIME. GET IT RIGHT, AND SAVE THE PAIN.

PREPARE
To get a close, comfortable shave, the hairs of the beard and mustache need to be soft. Heat and moisture get them that way. Ideally, you should shave after a hot shower. Failing that, holding a damp, steaming towel against your face for several minutes achieves almost equal results. Warmth also relaxes the skin, reducing the occurrence of nicks and razor burn.

LATHER
Apply a little shaving oil to the face before lathering. The blades will slide over it, cutting the hairs without touching the skin. Then lather up. We recommend using shaving cream from a tube for best results. With a badger-hair shaving brush, whip the cream into a rich froth with hot water in a shaving mug, then apply.

SHAVE
With proper preparation and an immaculate blade, two strokes of the razor are enough. First, draw the razor with the grain of the hair; this will remove about 80 percent of the whiskers. Then relather and make a return stroke against the grain, cleaning up the remainders. Always use a light touch, letting the blade, not pressure, do the work.

PROTECT
Rinse your face with cold water, then apply a moisturizing lotion. Do not use alcohol-based aftershaves, which dry the skin.

A SIMPLE GUIDE TO BODY-HAIR REMOVAL

BODY PART	NECESSARY	TOOL	HAZARDS	HOW OFTEN?
NOSE	Yes	Small scissors; electric nose-hair trimmer	With scissors, you could pierce your septum. Otherwise, none.	Check for errant hairs once a week and act accordingly
EAR	Yes	Shaving razor for lobe; small scissors	Inserting anything into your ear canal could lead to damage. Don't	As needed
BACK	Only if your back hair makes you uncomfortable. If not, leave it	Wax (administered by a professional); laser removal	Wax: Bursts of pain followed by horrendous acne breakouts. Laser: Debilitating pain, expensive	Once a year, six weeks before you'll take your shirt off in public
CHEST	Only if the hair becomes obtrusive	Small scissors or electric hair clipper	Cutting yourself; overtrimming your way back to early puberty	As soon as the hair becomes visible through a thin polo shirt
NETHER REGIONS	Not required but probably appreciated	Small scissors or electric hair clipper (keep the guard on and your eyes on the prize)	Too many to count, too horrible to name	Depends on how often someone is seeing it that isn't you

OUT-OF-CONTROL
EYEBROWS
What to do when your
eyebrows are growing like
kudzu

A lot of people think eyebrows are something you can take care of at home, but they're too easy to overdo, and you can end up looking worse than when you started. If you refuse to spend a couple of bucks getting threaded or plucked by a pro, at least heed their advice. First, get a good pair of tweezers. Be sure to get slanted tips; pointed tweezers are more likely to rip the hair or pinch your skin. The best time to pluck is right after a warm shower, when the hairs are easier to pull out. As for what to remove, put the pad of your thumb between your brows; whatever hair it covers needs to be gone. Carefully brush your brows up, and trim the hairs that stray over your brow line. As for shape, they should be proportional and neat, but not so neat as to look unnatural.

The ORIGINALS

HAIR APPARENT: JEAN-MICHEL BASQUAIT

During a short career ended by an untimely death, Basquiat managed to accomplish more than most people do in a lifetime. He broke barriers for Black artists, introduced graffiti to the art world, eclipsed Andy Warhol and Keith Haring, and become a style icon. Part of that last one is how he wore his hair, from half shaved to gravity-defying dreadlocks. Basquiat may have found success in the rarefied, and very white, New York art scene, but he never conformed to it or compromised himself for it. From Jay-Z to **the Weeknd**, artists are still paying homage to that legacy.

HOW TO USE
YOUR FACIAL HAIR

According to pogonologists (beard experts), the right facial hair can accentuate or minimize the features you were born with. Below are four examples of common problems, along with suggestions for using facial hair to fix them.

YOUR PHILTRUM IS HUGE

Solution: A relatively thick mustache will fill in the space (see fig. 1), or go with a long, full beard to even things out and draw attention away from that giant space between your nose and top lip.

YOUR FACE IS SKINNY

Solution: A short, scruffy beard will add some width, fill in your cheeks, and persuade any loitering raptors to move on.

YOUR FACE IS WIDE

Solution: Grow your beard, and square off the bottom to create the illusion of a strong chin. And let it grow down your neck at least an inch and a half.

YOUR FACE IS ROUND

Solution: An angular beard can add length and give your face a slimmer appearance.

Fig. 1

WHAT A CLOSE SHAVE FEELS LIKE

Every man should sit down for a professional shave at least once. For $20 to $60, you'll learn what can be achieved with a sharp blade in a steady hand. Until you do, read on. This is what a good shave is about: After the barber has finished with the shave—after he has draped your face with steamed towels of exquisite cotton; after he has applied a moisturizing gel to your mug; after he has covered you once more with the steamed towel; after he has brushed the powder into a rich foam on your chops and artistically removed your whiskers, first in one direction and then in the other (and it is artistic—a good Italian *barbiere* regards you as a sculptor regards his masterpiece, with eyes narrowed, appraisingly); after he has covered your face yet another time with a towel and briskly applied a tonic of your choosing—after all that, he takes the sheet with which he wrapped your face at the beginning of the process, folds it exactly once, and then uses it to fan that tonic and your smooth and restored face dry.

HOW TO SEAL THE DEAL
WITH A GOOD-LOOKIN' HANDSHAKE

DON'T CUT YOUR CUTICLES, that thin layer of skin that grows over the base of each nail. It's not sanitary, and it's not safe. Push them back with your fingertips after you shower, when your skin is softest.

SMOOTH THE EDGES. Nail files are important, and having your nails fully rounded will keep you from picking at them. Don't try to use the little file on your clippers—get a real one.

MOISTURIZE. Applying lotion daily can help prevent cracked and painful skin. Doing it at night will help avoid greasy hands during the day, but if you apply during sunlight hours, make sure the lotion has SPF.

LEAVE A LITTLE BIT OF WHITE at the tips of your nails. Cutting too close to the nail bed can cause infections and frustration when you find a spare penny. It's time to trim when you touch the end of your finger and can feel your nail.

STOP USING YOUR TEETH. Don't bite, chew, or gnaw on nails, hangnails, or cuticles. This is what separates us from animals. If you've got a hangnail, cut it away with a pair of sharp scissors.

POLISH? If you do, own it by picking a dark, neutral color that would go with most of the clothes you wear (navy, gray, black). They won't clash with most clothes and are subtle enough that some people may not even notice at first.

SKIN CARE 101: CLEANSE! EXFOLIATE! MOISTURIZE!

CLEANSE EVERY DAY. A good antibacterial soap works fine if you have oily skin. An alcohol-free (SD, denatured, and isopropyl) cream-textured cleanser is better if your skin is dry. Use warm, not hot, water—you want to open your pores gently, not scald them—and a washcloth, which is a better gunk remover than your bare hands.

EXFOLIATE ONCE A WEEK. It will remove the top layer of dead cells, which make your skin look dull and get rid of any deep-seated grime along with them. Use an exfoliating face scrub instead of your regular soap or cleanser. More frequent use will irritate your skin.

MOISTURIZE AND APPLY SUNSCREEN EVERY DAY. Always use a moisturizer with sunscreen, unless your skin is oily, in which case use a mildly astringent toner followed by an oil-free sunscreen. SPF 15 is more than adequate for the work environment, as long as you're not a lifeguard.

THE PERFECT
DOPP KIT*

To the untrained eye, it may look like other, nonperfect Dopp kits, but here's why it's perfect: It's made of nylon, so it's washable and suited to the messy rough-and-tumble of travel. Also, it's a shallow rectangle that you can stack in your bag. Finally, it's roomy enough to hold all of the following, which is more or less what every man should carry.

Airborne	Lint roller
Band-Aids	Lip balm
Body wash	Moisturizer-sunscreen combo
Deodorant	
Earplugs	Nail clippers
Extra pair of contact lenses	Razor
	Shaving cream
Floss	Shampoo
Ibuprofen	Toothbrush and toothpaste

A CRISP $20 BILL

What's that, you say? You've lost your wallet and have no access to cash? It's a good thing you've got a twenty-dollar bill tucked away in your Dopp kit. Plus, the bill measures six and one-eighth inches long, so you can use it to measure things—if you haven't already given it to the bellhop.

A WINE OPENER

Most accommodations provide one, but don't count on it. And there's no other way to get into that bottle that doesn't involve a gashed hand.

A SAFETY PIN

Use it to fasten a shirt if a button has popped, to pick an old-fashioned lock, to fix small tears, to fasten your pants if the zipper breaks, or to replace a lost screw in your sunglasses. The uses are myriad, but remember to fasten it so that the bulkier ends don't show.

YOUR WARDROBE

Good news—your closet doesn't need an overhaul. You just have to rethink some of your favorite pieces and mix in a few wisely selected new ones. It's all about finding fresh ways to wear the stuff you already love.

CONTINUED

"BUY LESS, BUY BETTER" has been a style dictum for a while, but it's taken on new meaning as we hurdle toward an uncertain future choked with stuff. We're all guilty of it: the shirt we already have four of, the pants that are appealingly different in the most insignificant way, the trend-adjacent outerwear that might not even see a second season. We know better, yet we still do it, the one more drink when we've already had plenty. Well, we're here to tell you that you can make better choices—for your style, your wallet, and the planet—and we can help.

It starts with some core essentials. An unstructured blazer, a pair of minimalist sneakers, the venerable Oxford shirt, some black lace-ups, a go-to suit. They don't need to be expensive—although the longer you hope to hold on to them the more investment worthy they are—but they need to work in almost any situation and they must fit perfectly. Keep in mind that basic isn't the same as bland. These are the styles you can wear day in and day out, but they're also meant to seamlessly work with your accessories, your third pieces (think of them like the spices you add to your cooking—they enhance), and those seasonal new pickups with a bit more swag. And once you have them you don't need to refresh your closet every year; in fact, we advise you don't. Instead, all you need to do is restock when time and wear warrant it (those white tees won't stay white forever). In the next few pages, we'll show you how to get there. But first, here are a few additional tips to keep in mind when creating a wardrobe that lasts.

PERFECT THE PATINA

There are two ways to be comfortable in your clothes. One: Forget about them. Two: Buy pieces that already look worn. Garment dyeing and garment washing—as central to Italian men's style as Parmesan is to food—give clothing a rumpled appearance, tone down bright colors, and deliver texture in spades.

EXPLORE THE DARK SIDE

Think fashion has gone off the deep end? Are you bombarded by garish graphics and look-at-me clothes? Sometimes the best remedy is to turn your back on it altogether and embrace the darkness. Black never goes out of style.

TOP IT OFF

High-low dressing used to mean tossing a blazer over something less dressy to create the perfect contrast. Today the concepts of formal and casual have blurred so much that the blazer can be replaced by a bomber, a leather jacket, a chore coat, or even just a cardigan.

LOWER THE MAINTENANCE

More and more, fabric innovations are ensuring that your clothes work harder than you do. Take washable wool suits, which make trips to the dry cleaner a thing of the past. Unstructured and elegant, they emerge pristine straight from the washing machine.

MAKE YOURSELF COMFORTABLE

Keeping things casual is the default nowadays (see chapter 7 for more on that). From suits to denim, the pieces that used to require some effort to get into or break in are now designed to fit comfortably right off the rack. From dress pants with elastic waists to added stretch in nearly everything (see our history of stretch on page 150), it's time to admit that no one needs to suffer for fashion.

BREAK THE RULES

Some guys think it's easiest to simply submit to the dress code. Sure—easy to forget. The rules of style have relaxed to the degree that, when done with self-confidence (not bravado), you don't even have to wear a shirt with a tux anymore. The determining factor is not your clothes but your attitude.

THE ESSENTIAL
WARDROBE

THE TEN THINGS YOU NEED IN YOUR CLOSET. YOU TAKE CARE OF THE SOCKS AND UNDERWEAR. FOLLOW OUR ADVICE ABOUT THE REST.

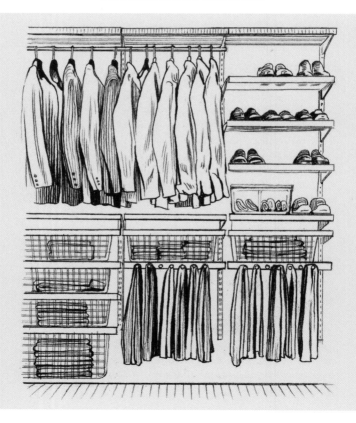

WHITE OXFORD BUTTON-DOWN SHIRT
The white button-down can be worn with a suit and tie, on its own with a pair of jeans, or underneath a sweater.

WHITE, GRAY, AND BLACK T-SHIRTS
Sleep in them, wear them on their own, or use them underneath a button-up or sweater.

LIGHTWEIGHT CASHMERE SWEATER
A thin cashmere sweater can be worn every month save summer's hottest days. Goes with jeans, chinos, cargo pants, suits, shorts, and more.

BLACK LACE-UPS
Clean, dressy black lace-up shoes will work with suits in any color and still look at home at the foot of your jeans.

SUNGLASSES
Obvious for their functionality (that whole sun-in-the-eyes thing) but also necessary as an accessory that adds the all-important final touch.

OVERNIGHT BAG
Because high-season hotels have that annoying two-night minimum, make sure it's big enough to carry a weekend's worth of stuff.

A DARK PAIR OF JEANS
Make sure they are crisp and able to be worn with a T-shirt, button-down, or any jacket in your closet.

TWO-BUTTON NAVY SUIT
Navy is the most versatile color for a man's suit. Extend its life by wearing it with a shirt and tie, or wear just the jacket with jeans and a button-down.

ONE SET OF CEDAR SHOE TREES
You need only one pair, to keep your just-worn shoes in good shape.

MEDIUM-WIDTH TIE
If it's too skinny or too fat, you limit the types of shirts you can wear with it. A medium width, in a neutral color and pattern, has the most versatility.

The ORIGINALS

CARY GRANT AND THE OFFICE SUIT

As with a few other great romantic stars, a wardrobe of superbly tailored clothes was an essential part of Cary Grant's mystique. The impeccable suits seemed like a second skin, as integral to his legendary presence as the cleft in his chin. Men wanted to be him, and the easiest way to do that was to dress like him. But times have changed, and even the professions that still require suits have relaxed the rules. Take the British royal family, for example. In another era, **Prince Harry** would be just as "suited and booted" as Grant, yet the expat prince prefers the open-collar look and off-the-rack suits.

BUILD A BUSINESS WARDROBE

THE 5 SHIRTS, 4 TIES, 3 SUITS, 2 SHOES, AND 1 OVERCOAT YOU NEED

These are the building blocks of a solid working wardrobe. Once you've got them covered, you can experiment with more colors and patterns. But start out with these essentials and you'll always be ready for the office. (See also Modern Office Style on page 152.)

5 SHIRTS

The shirt should have a supporting role in one's outfit. It's a backdrop—utility is paramount. Keep the color simple, and it will go with everything.

1 white Oxford cloth button-down, barrel cuff

1 blue or blue-and-white-stripe Oxford cloth button-down, barrel cuff

1 white spread collar, barrel cuff

1 white spread collar, French cuff

1 more shirt, not too ostentatious, that makes you feel good about yourself

4 TIES

Simple always looks sharpest.

1 plain navy (killer on a white shirt)

1 regimental stripe (bold but refined)

1 subdued paisley or pattern (for variety)

1 silk knit tie (for texture)

3 SUITS

Because you should never wear the same suit two days in a row.

1 navy two-button wool suit. Your most flexible investment, good for post-work and fine for the boardroom too.

1 charcoal flannel suit, single-breasted, two- or three-button

1 mid-gray glenurquhart or pinstripe, in lightweight wool

2 PAIRS OF SHOES

Because shoes need a day off, just like suits.

1 pair of plain black cap-toe oxford lace-ups, in calfskin. To get you through the day and well into the night.

1 pair of dark-brown derbies. They go with everything except a black suit, which you don't need anyway.

1 OVERCOAT

Well chosen, it's an investment that will last for years.

1 navy or black wool or cashmere fly-front overcoat, knee length and close fitting but never too tight.

UNLESS HE'S HEADED TO A BLACK-TIE WEDDING,
A MAN ALWAYS HAS OPTIONS

	DAYTIME BARBECUE	SUMMER COCKTAIL PARTY	DRINKING IN A BAR	HOLIDAY PARTY
Good	Chino shorts, solid tee, white canvas sneakers	Cotton chinos, camp collar shirt, minimal leather sneakers	Light-blue jeans, vintage T-shirt	Corduroy pants, crewneck sweater with a subtle pattern or texture
Better	Linen pants, polo shirt, leather slides	Lightweight suit, solid tee, loafers in suede or leather	Dark-blue jeans, long-sleeve rugby shirt	Tweed trousers, Oxford button-up, cashmere blazer or cardigan
Never	Jorts, tank top, flip-flops	Jeans (unless they're white) or patchwork madras (blazer or shorts)	Sweatpants, sport jersey	Holiday-themed anything, unless it's an "ugly sweater" party

The RULES

THINGS THE AMERICAN MAN CAN'T WEAR TO A FUNERAL: A bow tie, whimsical patterns, a light-colored coat, a silk pocket square, denim (unless the ceremony involves pouring out cans of Schlitz). At your own funeral? Wear whatever you please.

OFFICIALLY STATED DRESS CODES YOU CAN ALWAYS BEND: Black tie, business casual, casual.

OFFICIAL DRESS CODES YOU CAN'T: Cocktail formal, white tie, morning dress.

HOW TO DRESS FOR AN OCCASION

It's the hosts' rules that matter. If they have made no specific remarks on the invitation, go with convention. And then dress even better.

Anything that involves births, bar mitzvahs, marriages, or deaths requires your respect—even if you're not a believer in any of it. Religious ceremonies generally require a jacket.

For Islamic ceremonies, shoes are removed during prayer. Make sure you're wearing fresh, unholed socks. For Jewish ceremonies, especially if the congregation is Orthodox, don't be surprised if you're asked to wear a kippah (aka yarmulke).

Read the invite. If a wedding is in an unusual location, dress accordingly. Formal wear on a beach doesn't work (unless you're the groom). But if the setting is an official place of worship, wear a sober suit. A charcoal or dark navy suit will cover you for all eventualities.

The ORIGINALS

TRAVIS KELCE AND OCCASION DRESSING

The Kansas City Chiefs' tight end has had a monster few years: He's won three Super Bowls, he's famously dating Taylor Swift (as of today—stay tuned!), and he's become a bona fide style icon. From a date-night look that paired a matching, relaxed-fit corduroy jacket and pants to showing up to Super Bowl LVIII in a very shiny custom look by L.A.-based luxury designer Mike Amiri, Kelce has proved that his football, dating, and tunnel-walk skills are all at the superstar level.

A CONCISE GUIDE TO PATTERNS
REMEMBER WHEN YOUR GRANDFATHER USED TO WEAR PLAID ON PLAID? DON'T DO THAT.

BY THE BOOK	ALTERNATIVE

Keep it simple by pairing a minor color from your tie with a major color from your shirt. Similarly, you could match a major color on a tie with a minor shirt stripe.

Contrary to mainstream thinking, you can match a bold geometric tie with a striped shirt without inducing nausea. Don't be afraid to go very bold, in both color and the scale of the pattern.

For watches, concentrate on pairing color and material with your cuff links. Here it works because the shapes and colors complement each other perfectly. It would work equally well with a round, steel cuff link.

Pick a minor color from the pattern of your jacket and pair it with a watch that matches it in color—loosely. Then use the cuff link to create contrast. Avoid steel in favor of colored glass or silk knots. Don't try to match everything.

The utterly correct sock is one that is barely noticeable beneath the hem of your pants. (The pant legs here have been raised to show the socks.) The color should match your trousers to visually lengthen your legs.

Use your ankles as a place to add some color. Note that this works only if you maintain strict sobriety everywhere else in the outfit: plain black or very dark-brown shoes and little or no pattern anywhere else. But please, no novelty socks with dancing bananas or your dog's face. "Wacky socks guy" is not a personality.

SOME COLORS ARE MEANT TO BE TOGETHER. SOME ARE NOT.

BELOW, THE COMBINATIONS THAT DO AND DO NOT WORK

YES							
JACKETS	Brown	Gray	Black	Navy	Navy	Black	Brown
PANTS	Navy	Navy	Gray	Gray	Brown	Navy	Black
SHOES	Black	Brown	Black	Black	Brown	Black	Black
NO							
JACKETS	Brown		Gray		Black		Navy
PANTS	Black		Black		Brown		Black
SHOES	Brown		Brown		Black		Brown

THE DETAILS THAT SET YOU APART

WATCH
Think of it as a clear banner proclaiming your good taste, style, and success.

TIE
Should always be perfectly knotted, with a single notch or dimple and with the point sitting at the waistband.

CUFFS
Should show a quarter inch to a half inch past the jacket sleeve.

SHOES
Classic Italian, British, or American shoes.

HOW TO PULL OFF
SUMMER FABRICS

SEERSUCKER	COTTON	LINEN	SUMMER WOOL
The alternating puckered and smooth stripes keep the fabric off the skin and therefore, keep you a lot cooler. You probably first encountered it as the traditional blue-and-white suit, but these days it comes in black, olive, orange, and tie-dye. As shirting, shorts, swimwear, and even hats.	Humble cotton is everywhere because it is soft and breathable and can be made into everything from tees to suits. Look for Pima or Supima cotton fabrics since their longer fibers make for smoother, more durable fabrics. Extra points for garment-dyed cotton, whose rich colors wash down beautifully.	Linen is still the king of summer fabrics because nothing else matches its breathability (the secret is in the open weave, which allows for more airflow). It will cost you a bit more than cotton or seersucker, but in August you'll appreciate it. If you're going to own one summer suit, make sure it's linen.	Wool?! In the summer?! We know, we know, but trust us on this one because we don't like to sweat either. Wool is a miracle fiber that is almost unmatched at regulating temperature. The trick is to pick a "summer weight" with a looser weave. Do that and it's even cooler than cotton—for real.

HOW TO PULL OFF
WINTER FABRICS

CORDUROY	WAXED COTTON	GORE-TEX	TWEED
Corduroy is basically velvet with grooves cut into it that form the cords (wales) of the corduroy itself. It's also incredibly comfortable, and in its wider forms, warm too. It's also back in favor in a big way, so embrace it in trousers, shirting, blazers, and even down-filled outerwear.	You may not know a grouse from a partridge, but British hunting attire is a great introduction to waxed fabrics (they do know their crummy weather). A thin coating of water-repellent wax turns cotton into a winter fabric. And if hunting attire isn't your jam, you can now find waxed trucker jackets and barn coats.	The technical miracle can be found in plenty of jackets, but if you want to stay dry and warm, choose a Gore-Tex parka with a down fill. One that also has a trimmed hood will help keep whipping winds out, but make sure it's faux fur since the real stuff is a major faux pas these days.	Tweed is warm. Like really warm. That's reason enough to wear it during the winter. But it's also cool with its dusty image having been rehabbed by designers who are making all sort of stylish coats, shirt jackets, pants, and suits out of it. Look for labels using Harris Tweed, which is woven by hand.

HOW TO TRAVEL IN SUPERIOR STYLE

- Dress comfortably for air travel without completely losing your sense of good taste. Take a cue from NFL star Travis Kelce, who mixes a sensible white shirt on top with some baggy velour pants.

- Whether you plan to exercise while traveling or not, a pair of fashionable sneakers is the perfect travel shoe.

- Ensure your carry-on luggage is of sufficient quality and is well cared for—it gets scoped by your fellow passengers.

- A packable, unstructured blazer should be in your bag as much for unexpected formal-ish situations as when temps drop and you want to cover up in style.

- Having a lightweight, portable pillow can be a dream, especially if you get rebooked on a red-eye without notice.

- No matter where you're headed, having a button-down shirt on hand is a good idea. We suggest a classic Oxford cloth shirt—it is naturally wrinkle resistant and pairs well with almost anything.

WHAT TO PACK FOR THE CASUAL VACATION*

*Based on two nights and three days; does not include socks, underwear, or other small but vital travel items.

MOUNTAINS

FOR DAY: One anorak, two light sweaters, two T-shirts, one turtleneck, one pair of jeans, one pair of hiking boots, one pair of gloves.

FOR NIGHT: One dress shirt, one pair of dark corduroy pants, one wool blazer.
Don't even think about bringing: Bulky sweaters that overcrowd your suitcase.

BEACH

FOR DAY: Four T-shirts, two polo shirts, one pair of khaki shorts, one pair of swimming trunks, one pair of flip-flops.

FOR NIGHT: One pair of khaki pants, a crumpled-cotton unlined blazer, two dress shirts, one pair of loafers.
Don't even think about bringing: Your grape-smugglers, pineapple-print Hawaiian shirt.

PARIS

FOR DAY: One pair of jeans, one sweater, two T-shirts, one pair of comfortable walking shoes.

FOR NIGHT: One pair of trousers, two dress shirts, one pair of loafers, a navy blue lightweight wool blazer.
Don't even think about bringing: A beret and Breton stripe shirt.

THE DEFINITIVE STYLE RULES
LAYERING

1. Unless you live in Palm Springs, weather in fall and winter is rarely predictable. So take a cue from mountaineers: Three thin layers are better than one thick one.

2. The closer to your skin, the thinner the material.

3. A layer can be defined as any piece of clothing that can be worn with dignity on its own.

4. Your spring break T-shirt from sophomore year does not constitute a layer.

5. A layered combo should always include one piece of luxury, and for luxury, a tailored jacket will always do the trick.

6. But don't be afraid to shed that luxurious layer when the temperature begins to rise. Nobody likes the sweaty guy, no matter how cool his jacket is.

7. Just because Mother Nature is fond of dreary browns when the weather turns cold, that doesn't mean you have to be. Inject some color by way of a scarf or a sweater. Be fearless.

8. Casual doesn't have to mean jeans. Add some texture and personality below the belt with cords, chinos, or a pair of drawstring trousers.

9. If you can't put your arms all the way down at your sides, then your sweater is way too thick.

10. Layer just right and you can leave the coat at home.

THE ACTIVE MAN'S GUIDE TO HOSTILE WEATHER

1. Sunglasses aren't just for summer. The winter sun hangs low in the sky, which means glare. You can't duck to avoid what you can't see.

2. A good base layer, in either merino wool or polypropylene, is a lifesaver—sometimes literally—when temps drop below freezing.

3. Wind- and sunburn are no fun. Protect your skin and lips with SPF moisturizer and lip balm.

SWEATS ARE THE CENTER OF THE
CASUAL UNIVERSE

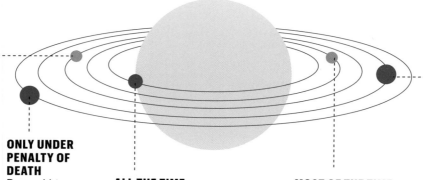

ONLY SOMETIMES
Hooded sweatshirt, matching sweatpants, high-top sneakers.

ONLY UNDER DURESS
Logo sweatpants, NBA jersey, flat brim hat.

ONLY UNDER PENALTY OF DEATH
Dress shirt, sweatpants, flip-flops.

ALL THE TIME
Hoodie, light-wash denim, retro sneakers.

MOST OF THE TIME
Graphic tee, sweatpants, technical sneakers.

The RULES

THERE IS A NAME FOR MEN WHO CAN PULL OFF WEARING SPORTS JERSEYS.
They're called professional athletes.

The ORIGINALS

JAY-Z AND AUTHENTIC STYLE

"You are now lookin' at the forty million boy/I'm rapin' Def Jam 'til I'm the hundred million man," Jay-Z predicted on 2001's *The Blueprint*. Today the rapper, luxury weed brand founder, record label and streaming service investor, designer, etc., etc. is worth somewhere north of $2.5 billion. Is it because he also embraced dressing up at a time when "keeping it real" in rap meant dressing down? It couldn't have hurt—it definitely helped solidify his rep as a serious business, man (that's not a typo. Jay once famously rapped, "I'm not a businessman, I'm a business, man"), and now he's the first billionaire in rap.

THE ULTIMATE CLOSET

HOW A MAN SHOULD ORGANIZE HIS WARDROBE

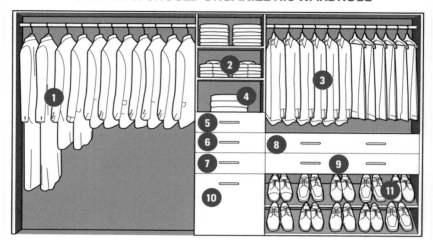

1. SUITS AND OVERCOATS
Hang three inches apart to minimize crushing.

2. EXTRA SHIRTS
If you're not planning on wearing them soon, fold and store on a shelf.

3. PRIMARY SHIRTS AND TROUSERS
Hang two inches apart to reduce creases.

4. SWEATERS
Fold in piles, and in the offseason, store in sealed containers.

5, 6 AND 7. SOCKS, UNDERWEAR, T-SHIRTS
Fold neatly.

8. TIES
Fold in half, then roll them up and place along with pocket squares and other accessories.

9. ATHLETIC CLOTHING
All in one place.

10. THICK KNITS AND SWEATSHIRTS
Store in deep drawers.

11. SHOES
Arrange on a shoe rack, making sure to dust unworn pairs every month.

THE CLOSET RULES

Don't overcrowd—stow seasonal items in a separate closet or storage space.

Your suit came in a bag for a reason—and not just to transport it home. A storage bag will protect it from pesky insects, fading, and dust.

Keep shoes in their bags and boxes to protect them from light and dust.

Fold knitwear such as sweaters on a shelf instead of hanging them. This will prevent stretching out the shape of the shoulders and neck.

Remove dry-cleaned items from wire hangers as soon as you get them home, and hang them on proper hangers. Thin wire hangers will eventually stretch the clothes hung on them—and they're ugly.

KNOW YOUR ENEMY: MOTHS

The casemaking clothes moth (*Tinea pellionella*) and the common webbing clothes moth (*Tineola bisselliella*) are probably already living in your home, hungrily eyeing your wool suits and sweaters. Instinct suggests that killing them will take care of the problem. But it's the moth larvae, not the adults, that do the actual damage. They feed on keratin, a natural protein found in wool, cashmere, mohair, silk, and leather. They're also virtually invisible—so even if you see no adult moths in your closet, that doesn't mean you don't have a problem. How best to solve it?

Laundering and dry cleaning both destroy moth eggs and larvae. Emptying and airing the contents of your wardrobe regularly is also advisable. And vacuuming prime moth hideouts—along baseboards, in closets, under furniture, and along carpet edges—will help rid your home of adults. Dry-clean or wash all wool items before you put them away. For long-term storage—sweaters in summer, lightweight suits in winter—Space Bags or other tight-sealing containers are ideal. Mothballs are just regrettable.

A FIELD GUIDE TO HANGERS

General purpose, dependable support

For sport coats only

For trousers only, by the hem

For suits only

For breaking into your car

THE TOOLS
EVERY MAN NEEDS IN HIS WARDROBE

THE BELT-HOLE PUNCH
If you need it only once, it pays for itself.

THE CLOTHES BRUSH
A friend to your suits. Removes stuff you didn't even know was there.

THE CLOTHES SHAVER
Used sparingly, an effective way to remove pilling from expensive sweaters.

COLLAR STAYS
Save the spare collar stiffeners you get when you buy a shirt in a small box. Collar stays get bent out of shape in the wash and often need replacing.

DRAWERS OR SHELVES FOR KNITWEAR
Because they'll last much longer folded flat and laid on a shelf than stuck on a hanger.

A GOOD STEAM IRON
Invest in lots of temperature settings, a steam release, and water-spray buttons.

HANGERS
The right shape for the right garment (see page 205).

AN IRONING BOARD
Because you need something to use the steam iron on.

LINT REMOVER
The quick self-adhesive solution to visible fluff, pet hair, and dandruff.

THE PROFESSIONAL STEAMER
The best investment you can make—you'll save yourself a fortune in dry-cleaning bills (see page 208).

THE SEAM RIPPER
Use this ingenious tool to remove troublesome labels and unpick pocket-basting thread.

THE SHOE-CLEANING KIT
A buffing cloth, some polish, and a couple of brushes. See page 100 for polishing instructions.

THE SHOEHORN
Your shoes will be much better off in the long run.

SHOE TREES
Maintain the shape of your shoes. Will triple their life span.

A SLEEVE BOARD
A mini ironing board to get those shirtsleeves looking immaculate.

A SMALL BOX IN A DRAWER FOR BITS AND PIECES
Stores cuff links, studs, and watches safely in one place.

SPACE BAGS
Something you can use to seal against the elements and bugs (see page 205).

STITCH WITCHERY
A white-tape wonder that you iron under your trouser hems for short-term take-up solutions.

SUIT BAGS
For hanging your more expensive clothing when it's not being worn. Obsessive? No, sensible.

THE RULES OF PACKING

FOR SMALL SUITCASES

Store your miscellaneous gadgets in an old Dopp kit. It will protect them and keep them all in one place.

Save space and save your tie's integrity by rolling it up and placing it safely inside one of your shoes. This is also a great way to store socks.

Sweaters, especially cashmere, should be folded and laid to the width of the suitcase to prevent bunching and wrinkling.

FOR MIDSIZE BAGS

Your Dopp kit should be slim and shallow and contain travel-size toothpaste.

Place your lightest pair of shoes at the bottom of your bag. Wear your heaviest; it will leave your bag lighter.

Roll small items such as underwear and T-shirts tightly, then use them to hold everything else in your bag in place.

FOR LARGE SUITCASES

Turn your suit jacket inside out. The inner lining, now on the outside, will protect it from wrinkling.

Fold the jacket in on itself along the center of its back, then once more, until you've folded it into quarters.

Wrap the suit in dry-cleaning plastic at the bottom of the suitcase, so it will not move around and crease.

HOW MANY TIMES CAN I WEAR IT
BETWEEN WASHES?

ITEM	ACCEPTABLE WEARINGS	BUT ...
Jeans	5 to 10	Fewer if they get visibly dirty or baggy at the knee
Sweater	10 to 15	Chunkier knits can survive many more
Sweatshirt	2	Weekends don't count
T-shirt	1	But two if it's an old favorite
Dress shirt	1	But two (nonconsecutively) in a real pinch
Underwear	1	But nothing
Socks	1	See underwear, above
Suit	Hundreds, if not thousands	Only if you brush, steam, and air regularly
Coat	Hundreds, if not thousands	Only if you dry-clean sparingly, store properly, and repair as-needed

THE ENDORSEMENT
THE CLOTHES STEAMER

There's a simple tool that can slash your cleaning bills, lengthen your suit's life by several years, and ensure that you always step out the door looking immaculate. It's called a steamer, and you need one. Most natural fibers in suit cloths are susceptible to creasing and bagging in areas of movement (elbow, crotch, knees). Steam works on them like a sauna does on humans, allowing them to relax and regain their natural shape. Unlike harsh cleaning and hot pressing, steam rarely has ill effects. Spend fifty dollars on a steamer and it will pay for itself in six months from the savings on your cleaning bill alone. The technique is simple. Arrange the jacket or trousers on a hanger (ideally one that allows you to work the entire length of the leg in a single stroke). Switch on the steamer, and wait until a steady emission of steam develops. Then move the head of the steamer over the cloth in an up-and-down motion, keeping it about two inches from the fabric at all times. The creases will drop out in a matter of seconds, leaving your suit looking as good as new.

DRY-CLEANING:
THE TRUTH

Between the solvents, mechanical agitation, and high drying temperatures, a good suit in the wrong hands can quickly become a thrift shop donation. To protect your investment, choose your dry cleaner wisely. Ask a trusted tailor or retailer for a recommendation.

Clean your suits as infrequently as possible and you'll lengthen their life. Unstained suits can be cleaned once per season and lightly pressed or steamed between wearings. But use good judgment: Everyday buildup from dirt, sweat, and cologne can discolor and deteriorate garments, and pressing these contaminants into an item will make the grime permanent.

IF YOU WITNESS THESE SIGNS, IT'S TIME TO FIND A NEW CLEANER

Puckering or bubbling: Threads in garments cleaned at the wrong temperature can shrink, warping the fit.

Shininess: Hard pressing can crush fabric fibers and cause a glossy appearance.

Indentations: Improper pressing may also leave imprints around pockets and buttons.

TO LENGTHEN TIME BETWEEN CLEANINGS

Use a steamer (see opposite page).

Air out jackets and pants for a few hours before returning them to your closet, so you don't trap moisture.

The old trick of hanging your suit near the shower for a light steam will save you trips to the cleaners.

ANOTHER REASON TO ROTATE YOUR WARDROBE

Giving the suit a few days to hang and relax will help restore its shape.

The RULES

ALMOST ALWAYS BLOT RATHER THAN RUB. Rubbing damages the fibers, removes dyes, and can spread or set the stain.

ACT QUICKLY. The less time the stain sits, the better your odds of saving your shirt. Know your limits. You might do more harm than good with oil-based stains. Find a dry cleaner.

ESQUIRE'S OLD-FASHIONED
GUIDE TO DIY STAIN REMOVAL

PRODUCT	FOR	HOW
Aspirin	Sweat stains	Drop two pills in water, and soak stain in solution.
Baking soda	Coffee	Add water to make a paste. Apply, let dry, then rinse.
Borax	Anything	Follow package directions.
Club soda	Anything	Sponge onto wet stain, and dry with towel.
Clorox Bleach Pen	Anything	Follow package directions.
Cream of tartar	Chili sauce	Mix with lemon juice, apply, and launder.
Dish soap	Anything	Rub onto stain and rinse.
Cornstarch	Grease	Apply to stain. Let dry.
Glycerin	Mustard	Apply to stain, let sit, and rinse.
Gold Bond powder	Grease	Sprinkle on stain, let dry, brush off, and wash.
Hair spray	Ink	Spray onto stain, let dry, and wash
Hydrogen peroxide	Blood	Apply directly to stain and launder
Lemon	Rust	Squeeze onto stain, add salt, and launder
Liquid dishwasher detergent	Anything	Pour on stain and let sit for ten minutes. Wash
Nail-polish remover	Nail polish	Apply to stain, let sit, and rinse
OxiClean stain remover	Anything	Follow package directions
Rubbing alcohol	Grass	Sponge on and wash.
Salt	Red wine	Sprinkle on wet stain, let dry, and brush off.
Shampoo	Soiled shirt collar	Brush on and launder.
Shortening	Tree sap	Mix fifty-fifty with water.
White vinegar	Salt	On light fabrics, sponge onto stain and wash.

THE ESQUIRE GUIDE TO

LONGEVITY

The responsibilities start the moment you take a new piece of clothing home. It's up to you how long it's going to last.

THE DEFINITIVE KEY TO CARE LABELS

1. JEANS
Wash your jeans inside out to preserve the indigo dye on the surface and the structure of cotton fibers. ADD 2 YEARS.

2. SWEATERS
Wash wool and cashmere by hand using only knitwear-specific detergents, like Woolite. Dry flat, spreading the sweater out. ADD 2 YEARS.

3. TIES
Roll your untied ties rather than hang them. Then the running stitch that constitutes the spine of the tie can relax. ADD 5 YEARS.

4. SHIRTS
Never dry-clean. Have them laundered and hand ironed if possible. Less pressing means less wear and tear. ADD 2 YEARS.

5. SHOES
Own at least three good pairs for work. Never wear a pair more than twice a week. Use shoe trees. ADD 20 YEARS.

6. SUITS
Store your out-of-season suits in airtight bags. ADD 5 YEARS.

7. SUITS
Brush them regularly to remove lint in hidden areas, like armpits, that can attract moths. ADD ANOTHER 2 YEARS.

8. SUITS
Steam regularly to remove creases between annual dry cleaning. ADD 10 YEARS.

What it means: Hand-wash.
What it really means: Wash in warm water (between 90 and 105 degrees) mixed with detergent. Don't scrub too hard.

What it means: Do not iron.
What it really means: Use a steamer to work out the wrinkles, or take it to a dry cleaner.

What it means: Do not tumble dry.
What it really means: Drape the washed garment over a clothesline or a dry, clean surface that won't warp the garment's shape. Let dry.

What it means: Do not bleach.
What it really means: Check your laundry detergent's ingredients for bleach's chemical name, sodium hypochlorite.

What it means: Dry-clean.
What it really means: Always take delicate fabrics like silk to a dry cleaner. You can hand-wash some stuff yourself, but it's risky.

What it means: Machine wash.
What it really means: Number of dots indicates temperature. One is cold.

THE
APPENDIX

SIZING GUIDE

LIKE BOXING, FITTING CLOTHES IS AN INEXACT SCIENCE whose variables can be attributed to the glorious fact that no two bodies are exactly alike. For that matter, despite supposedly standard, ready-to-wear sizing, it's difficult to find two garments that are cut and sewn precisely the same way, which is less glorious, but equally germane. (Ready-to-wear, or off-the-rack, refers to garments made in factories or workshops in a range of standard sizes.) When you add the fact that there are different sizing systems in different parts of the world, finding the right size becomes even more complicated. That's why a good tailor is worth his weight in Japanese silk.

CALCULATING YOUR MEASUREMENTS

The instructions that follow describe how to measure yourself correctly and, in turn, determine your general sizes in various garments and in shoes. A convenient thing about your body is that you always have it with you (you do try on everything before you buy it, right?) But if your girlfriend has offered to pick up something for you on her next business trip to London, be sure she has your exact measurements. Regardless of who's buying, use the conversion charts on the following pages as guidelines rather than decrees. These instructions describe how a tailor would measure you. You can also find a garment you own that fits you really well, and measure its corresponding parts.

CHEST
Wrap the tape measure under your armpits, around the fullest part of your chest and shoulder blades. Don't flex, but breathe in first.

NECK
Measure around the base of your neck, about an inch below your Adam's apple. Slip two fingers inside the tape to ensure comfort.

SLEEVE
Hold your arm out straight from your side (not in front of you) at a 45o angle to the body. Ask someone to measure from your shoulder joint to your wristbone.

WAIST
Wrap the tape measure around your trunk where your belt normally goes, about one to two inches below the navel. Keep the tape measure a little loose, or put a finger between your body and the tape measure.

INSEAM
You'll need a friend, preferably someone you really like and trust, to measure your inner leg from just shy of the family jewels to your anklebone.

OUTSEAM
This one's easier. Hold the tape to the top of your waistband on the outside of the leg (or where the waistband would fall) and have someone measure the distance to the bottom of your ankle, or where you want the trouser leg to end. Measure each leg separately.

FOOT (SHOE SIZE)
Sit with your foot (in a sock) on a piece
of paper with your shinbone at a slightly forward angle, and trace around your foot with a pencil. Draw parallel lines to mark outermost points (width length) of your foot. Measure the length to A/af of an inch. Do the same with your other foot. Choose the larger foot and subtract A/af to V of an inch from the measurement to allow for error.

HAT
With a tape measure, form a loop around the back of your head, tape parallel to floor, about an inch and a half above your ears, meeting at the center of your forehead.

GLOVE
Measure a loop around the widest part of your hand, where the calluses form under your index finger and pinky.

SIZE CONVERSIONS

SUITS AND JACKETS
Standard sizing is based on the chest measurement. For additional guidelines, see pp. 38–39.

Letter	US/UK (in)	Europe
XXS	32	42
XS	34	44
S	36	46
M	38	48
M	40	50
L	42	52
XL	44	54
XL	46	56
XXL	48	58

DRESS SHIRTS
Standard sizing is based on the neck measurement. Most dress shirts also come in different sleeve lengths.

US/UK (in)	Europe
14	36
14½	37
15	38
15½	39
16	41
16½	42
17	43
17½	44
18	45

TROUSERS

Standard sizing is based on the waist measurement. Jeans and some dress trousers often also include an inseam measurement.

US (in)	28	30	32	34	36	38	40	42	44	46	48	50
Euro	44	46	48	50	52	54	56	58	60	62	64	66
cm	71	76	81	86	91	97	102	107	112	117	122	127

SHOES

Many shoes, and most dress shoes, come in different widths, ranging in the United States from AAA to EEE, though these are far from standardized.

US	UK	Euro	Asian
6.5	5.5	39	23.5
7	6	40	24.5
7.5	6.5	40	24.5
8	7	41	25.5
8.5	7.5	41 / 42	25.5
9	8	42	26.5
9.5	8.5	43	27.5
10	9	43/44	27.5

US	UK	Euro	Asian
10.5	9.5	44	28.5
11	10	44	28.5
11.5	10.5	45	29.5
12	11	46	30.5
12.5	11.5	46/47	30.5
13	12	47	31.5
13.5	12.5	47/48	31.5
14	13	48	32.5

HATS

Letter	Inches	US	Metric
XS	20 3/8	6 1/2	52
XS	20 3/4	6 5/8	53
S	21 1/4	6 3/4	54
S	21 1/2	6 7/8	55
M	22	7	56

Letter	Inches	US	Metric
M	22 3/8	7 1/8	57
L	23 1/4	7 1/4	58
L	23 3/8	7 3/8	59
XL	23 1/2	7 1/2	60
XL	24	7 5/8	61

GLOVES

Inches	Standard	Military
6.5 - 7	7 - 7.5	3
7.5 - 8	8 - 8.5	4

Inches	Standard	Military
8.5 - 9	9 - 10	5
9.5 - 10	10.5 - 11	6

INDEX

CREDITS

HEARST
HOME

Copyright © 2024 by Hearst Magazine Media, Inc.
All rights reserved.

Cover and book design by Gino Chua
Text by Michael B. Dougherty

Library of Congress Cataloging-in-Publication
Data Available on request

10 9 8 7 6 5 4 3 2 1

Published by Hearst Home, an imprint of Hearst
Books/Hearst Magazine Media, Inc.
300 W 57th Street
New York, NY 10019

Esquire, Hearst Home, the Hearst Home logo, and
Hearst Books are registered trademarks of Hearst
Communications, Inc.

For information about custom editions, special
sales, premium and corporate purchases: hearst.
com/magazines/hearst-books

Printed in China
978-1-958395-80-6

Scan the QR code for the latest news from Esquire
about men's fashion, including style advice, trends,
and grooming tips.